Your Money, *Your* Values

How You Can
Align Your
Investments with
Your Values

^{BY} Stephen R. Bolt

VFN Publishing
Nashville, Tennessee

Your Money, Your Values

Published by
Values Financial Network, Inc.
2505 21st Avenue South, Suite 204
Nashville, Tennessee 37212

Cover Design by
LYNETTE HOWARD/LY Designs
Nashville, Tennessee

Editorial and Layout Services by
Guardian Angel Communications Services,
Nashville, Tennessee

Printed by
Vaughan Printing
Nashville, Tennesse

Dedication

*This book is dedicated to the
Founding Fathers of this great republic,
who had the courage to care enough
about their values
that they sacrificed everything
to ensure that we would always
be able to express ours.*

Table of Contents

— SECTION II —
Values-based Investment Management

— SECTION III —
Integrating Values into Your Financial Plan

Acknowledgements

As is probably the case with most books, so many people played a role in assisting me in the writing, printing, and distribution of this book that there is insufficient space here to give them each proper thanks. There are a few, however, whose assistance became so vital that without their help the book simply could not have been printed in a timely manner.

My compliments to Mason Rodgers and David Prentice for their fortitude and tenacity in arranging for the editing, layout, and printing of *Your Money, Your Values*.

I also want to thank Ambassador Rodgers, Lynda, Preston, Larry, Mike, Andy, Mark, and Jason for catching the vision and helping me add flesh to the entire project. A very special thanks I also give to my good friend Patrick Johnson whose resource material and personal assistance became invaluable.

I thank also my staff, particularly Amy Yokley and Ginger English, for both their prodding and support, as well as their assistance in organizing the information.

I am grateful to my wife, Libby, and our two daughters, Ruby and Ann-Rachel, for allowing me yet another project that invariably reduces the time and energy I am able to devote to them.

Finally, I want to thank the pioneers of the SRI industry for exploring, developing and implementing ways that people can express their personal values and convictions in how they invest their money.

Stephen R. Bolt

Foreword

By Michael V. Williams

The amount of information available today and the speed with which we can access it is, indeed, amazing. The cyber world is affecting the way we live and how we do business. In the financial services industry, it is certainly changing the nature of the relationship between an investor and his or her advisor. The information boom is increasing the level of investor sophistication and available choices.

Values-based investing is one of those new dynamics that is reshaping this industry. The term value-added continues to surface in our industry. It is no longer, however, just a cliché but an essential ingredient in a financial practice as a deliverable in a successful client-advisor relationship. There are, of course, a number of ways to bring value-added to a relationship. My friend Stephen Bolt, in *Your Money, Your Values*, shares with us, what is to me, the cornerstone of value-added. What better way of establishing the foundation of a life plan can there be than beginning with a reflection of your values in your investment decision-making process?

I feel certain that values-based investing will make an impact on your life—it has on mine. Stephen's book is a tremendous tool in providing us with vital information on values-based investing, as well as a practical method of applying your values to your investments.

I've been in this industry for over twenty-seven years, and I believe Stephen's book on values-based investing is one of the most meaningful and timely works for the financial services industry and the clients we serve.

Thank you, Stephen, for your vision, commitment, and for what seems like an endless source of energy to make a difference.

Michael V. Williams is a Senior Executive of one of the largest financial services companies in the world. His vast experience in "consultative selling" is helping to substantially and positively transform the way financial services are delivered.

Letter to the Reader

Dear Reader,

Thank you for taking the time and energy to obtain this copy of *Your Money, Your Values*. I hope that you find the information contained in this unique book inspirational, educational, and most of all, useful.

Over the years I have traveled a great deal. I use my air time to read. A couple of years ago I found myself reading a number of self-help books. The information was generally quite interesting and one book tended to lead me to another, and so on. Finally, I picked up a book in one of the airport book stores and opened it to the introduction. The author's remarks caught me completely off guard with an admonition that hit me in the heart! He said something like, "If you have read a number of self help books, please close this book and put it back on the shelf. This one, like the others that you have read, contains much good information that is designed to help you change your life. But that information is only good to the extent that you apply it. Reading it may be interesting, but in the final analysis, if you don't act on it, the book is worthless."

Your Money, Your Values contains information that can change your life. Much of it is simply not available in any other book on the market today. I encourage you to commit to applying the part of this book that is appropriate to you.

Most people will want to talk with a financial services professional after reading this book. As you consider developing a professional relationship with an advisor keep in mind that a national network of financial services professionals has been established to help people integrate their personal values with their money. The advisor affiliated with the Values Financial Network has been specifically trained on values-based investing and can answer many, if not all, of your questions.

I would like to hear from you, too. Please contact me at http://www.VFNinfo@VFN.net and let me know if you found the book useful. If you talk with a member of the VFN, please let me know if you found that helpful as well. Your feedback is very important to us.

Again, thank you for taking the time and having the interest to read *Your Money, Your Values*. My hope is that this book will help you live a more purposeful, spiritual and fulfilling life.

Stephen Bolt

Introduction

As I made my last step up the hill and out onto the precipice, heart racing much more from fear than high altitude, I was immediately hit by a blast of ice cold January wind making its way through the New Mexico mountains.

For the preceding thirty-four torturous hours, I had visualized how I would make myself go through with this—a zip line almost 500 feet above a rocky, snow-covered stream below. Far out into my field of vision I could see my teammates who were waiting for me, to pull me in. My gosh! They must be a half mile away! They look so small from up there. But no matter. I'll be done with this in a flash.

I had rehearsed the sequence over and over again. The Executive Training Curriculum I was engaged in presented both classroom and field exercises. All of the field exercises appealed to me—climbing up the side of a wall, jumping into oblivion from the precarious top of a telephone pole, falling backwards into my teammates' arms with eyes closed—all of these were "fun" to me. But not the zip line.

For some reason, the idea of voluntarily jumping off of a 500-foot cliff holding on to nothing but a little bar attached to a pulley (*okay, there was a harness*), free falling for a few seconds until the line became taught, then zipping across at mach speed until one eventually found the flailing arms of my comrades was an excruciatingly anxious proposition for me. But I had no choice in the matter, because I was one of the managers—a leader! So I devised a plan....

I decided that I would keep my mind on something else as we scaled the back side of the small mountain. My pace would keep me concerned only with my task—and breathing the thin 8000-foot, oxygen-depleted air. Once on top, I would not even glance at the challenge in front of me, but instead concentrate on helping my assistants' efforts at "belting" me in to my harness. Then, without so much as a cursory look past my shoes, I would...jump. Whether I lived or died, at least it would be over and it would be over quickly. No anguish, no real fear, just "activity"—a process—then it's over.

So, as I stepped out onto the precipice, all was going as planned. My helpers stationed there harnessed me in and checked the pulley. They looked at me and said, "Okay, you're good to go!" Given my send off, I pushed my foot forward, only to find something holding me back. I looked over my shoulder to find the young, dark-haired assistant on my right holding on to one of my straps. I looked at him incredulously, and he smiled with one of those "I-know-what-you're-trying-to-do-but-I'm-not-going-to-let-you-get-away-with-it" grins. He pulled me back the twelve inches I had successfully negotiated and said, "Stop! Take a deep breath. Now, I want you to look straight ahead. You see those friends of yours waaaaay out there?"

I swallowed real hard and uttered, "Yes."

He looked left and asked, "You see those trees way over there down that gorge?"

All I could do was nod. Then he turned to the right and said, "Look at those lights way down there. That's the lodge. Do you see it?"

Of course I did. By now it had been a solid five minutes since I was positioned perilously on that precipice—well past my plan, and well past my tolerance!

As if I wasn't in enough panic, my "helper" then looked *down*. He said, "Look at the stream down there. If you look closely, you can see the movement of the water."

Okay, I was toast! My heart rate was seriously past the bursting point; my emotional state was beyond repair!

At that point, he slowly, very slowly, began moving behind me, pulling his hand away from my strap. He looked at me and said proudly, "Now you are ready. Go whenever you choose."

I'll never forget that experience. It was, of course, a metaphor for life. We tend to rush through so many of life's tasks, just to "get it over with," that we fail to appreciate the totality of the experience. Had I been allowed simply to run off that cliff without so much as a glance at the ground so ominously far down below, the zip line would have been nothing more than a "ho hum" experience. Instead, I was forced to face my fear, make a choice (to go, or not to go), and appreciate the consequences.

Several years ago, I watched a television special on the life of Marlon Brando. The program took the audience through Brando's incredible life—Hollywood and hobnobbing with kings, queens, and presidents; the French Riviera; yachts; and an endless social life. It was an amazing story of what, by most peoples' standards, was a very full and rich life.

At the end of the program, the interviewer turned to Brando and asked a most interesting question, "Let's say that you were on your deathbed and you had only minutes to live. Thinking back over your incredible life, how would you sum it all up?"

Marlon Brando looked away in thought and then answered, "Whew! What was that all about?"

I burst out laughing. To this day, I smile when I think about his response. On the other hand, however, it is a profoundly sad explanation for one's own life. I think Marlon Brando realized toward the twilight of his life what so many others only then begin to appreciate. Real life is not about narcissism. It's not about accumulated wealth, popularity, or fame. Rather, life is about purpose and meaning, and those who get that right are able to have a total life experience, deep and rich, which extends well beyond the boundaries of self and death.

In our world today, it is profoundly unfortunate that the developing consensus seems to be summed up with, "I can't do anything about it, so I'll just live my life and go with the flow," The "it" that people seem to think they have so little control over ranges from taxes, to the judicial system and politics in general, to the environment, military and nuclear power. But the truth is that never before in the history of the world has so much power been given to the individual, particularly in the United States.

This book is the first of its kind. Its purpose is both simple and profound: to help individuals appreciate and exercise the enormous power they have as citizens of a democratic republic to change their world. Although the power that I will show has been available to many throughout history, with the advent of technology and, particularly, a highly successful economy, never before have so many been in a position to create the world that they choose for themselves, their family, and others.

The recipe for the "power to change your world" rests in the proper synergistic composition of three distinctly different elements: values, money, and technology. *Your Money, Your Values* is written as a practical guide to show you how to engage these three disparate dynamics that you use every day of your life in a way that will add new and profound meaning to your life.

You have the power to affect your world right now. You probably just hadn't thought about it the way we will present it. But without really thinking about, you'll end up rushing right through the process called life.

But now that you've picked up this book, as your personal "helper" standing with you on that precipice, I am asking you to, "Stop! Look around. To your left, to your right, and especially *down*. There is a lot going on around you that either you have intentionally disregarded, or have felt unable to contribute toward a solution that was meaningful. Take a deep breath, learn how to use the power that you have, and then go... whenever you're ready."

Section I

The Values Proposition

Values-based investing
is the process of integrating
one's belief system into
personal investment decisions
to achieve both
financial and social return.

CHAPTER 1

Values-based Investing Explained

Adam walked into the house, satisfied with having just completed a successful campaign on behalf of the local Crisis Pregnancy Center. For a number of years, Adam had served on the board of the center after he had been convicted on the abortion issue as a teenager. He had gone "too far" with his girlfriend, and she had gotten pregnant.

For help, Adam prayed, talked with his pastor and, finally, his parents. After talking with people he respected, Adam decided to marry his girlfriend and give the child a proper family. Unfortunately, his girlfriend had no interest in his marriage proposal. And even more shocking to Adam, she also had no interest in carrying the child to term.

So Adam sat helplessly as his girlfriend received counseling and then an abortion through the local Planned Parenthood facility.

Although that experience happened ten years ago, the memory still haunts Adam. Shortly thereafter, Adam decided to do everything in his power to support others who were suddenly in the frightening position of an unplanned pregnancy. He hoped that he could help them protect the life that they were given, whether intentional or not.

One day Adam walked to the refrigerator and poured a diet soda while browsing through his unopened mail. One of the envelopes contained a quarterly report from a mutual fund company where Adam had a small IRA. He opened it and pulled out the contents. As usual, this report was filled with performance figures, a comprehensive report to shareholders from the fund manager, and his individual account statement. As he took a drink from his glass, Adam noticed a "Listing of Key Holdings" in the report. He just about choked on his soda as he recognized one of the companies in which stock was held by his IRA mutual fund. It was a national company with high name recognition, and one with strong ties to Planned Parenthood.

Adam couldn't believe it! He had devoted thousands of hours as a volunteer to support the life of the unborn. Yet at the same time, he was giving his investment dollars to a company that, in turn, gave financial support to Planned Parenthood.

Suddenly Adam felt like a hypocrite, a fake, and an imposter. He also felt like going to the telephone and demanding an immediate redemption of all his money held in that mutual fund. But Adam had a problem.

Before he could make the call to liquidate his investment in that fund, he first had to find out where he could invest his money in a mutual fund that would reflect his values and not those of Planned Parenthood. After all, he thought, it was his money and it should reflect his values. What assurance would he have that the next values-indiscriminate mutual fund wouldn't run the same risk?

Adam's story is not unique. Millions of investors each year face the same quandary. Many people have told me things like, "I watched my father die a horrible death from lung cancer after years of smoking. I don't care where you invest my money, I just don't want any of it to find its way into the tobacco industry."

Whether your personal values are strongly related to affirmative action, pornography, gambling, the environment, nuclear power or another issue, you should have the opportunity to "vote with your money." That is to say, leverage your money in support of your values.

WHAT IS VALUES-BASED INVESTING?

Our world is changing at a pace unprecedented in human history. Technology that was supposed to give us more time to relax has instead simply increased the pace of our lives. Information that only a few decades ago used to be delivered once a day in the form of a local newspaper is now produced in seconds and delivered over multiple electronic media.

This new world has created a global community that is smaller and closer, and at the same time, one that has fostered a desire for greater individualism. Cultural, political, and religious diversity has never been more prevalent, even though we all have become part of a "one world" economic and telecommunications network. There is a resurgence of interest in personal values and spirituality. We want to "make a difference," and we express that desire in new and impactful ways.

Nowhere is that expression more obvious than in the new world of investing. The ability to attain both a financial return and a moral return on an invested dollar is nothing short of revolutionary. *Values-based investing is the process of integrating one's belief system into personal investment decisions to achieve both financial and social return.* It is the process of aligning your investment assets with deeply held personal values in order to create a double bottom line.

There are two primary motivations for individuals to choose values-based investing:

- **Personal Integrity**—the desire to align every area of one's life with one's value system...a holistic world-view based on values.

- **Corporate Change**—the desire to create positive corporate change in line with one's personal values.

If you think about it, you currently reflect your values in many areas of your life. For example, the church you attend and the political party you support both are reflections of who you are as an individual and how you reflect your values. But have you ever thought about how your everyday financial decisions are influenced by your values?

Think about charities for a moment. Both the amount of money you give to charitable organizations, and the type of charitable organizations you support are the direct result of your internal value system. If one of your family members has struggled with gambling, and you have witnessed firsthand the devastating consequences of this struggle, then this will influence your thinking about gambling and help shape your values on that particular industry. When you consider which charitable organizations to support, you may give special consideration to organizations that seek to combat the gaming industry. Your financial support is therefore a direct expression of your values.

But let's carry it a bit deeper with regard to financial decisions by looking at your spending. It has been said that if you want to find out what a person truly values most, simply take a look at that person's checkbook. People can put up a good front and "fool some of the people some of the time" with regard to their values. However, if you look at their spending decisions, you'll often see that the choices they make in everyday life often go against the personal values projected.

It has amazed me many times that some political candidates who consistently portray themselves as a "champion of the people" often spend so little of their personal financial resources helping others through charitable donations. For example, remember the public and media outcry a few years ago when then-Vice President Al Gore released his federal tax return, revealing that less than 1 percent of his and Tipper's income was given to charity? This is a classic example of discovering where a person's values really lie.

On the other hand, values-based investing is extending the same values you reflect in your giving and spending decisions into your investment decisions. Let's consider the gambling example in light of values-based investing. Since your values on gambling are shaped by your beloved family member who has struggled with a gambling problem, you would never go to a casino and spend your money to support the industry. You may even give a percentage of your financial resources to charitable organizations that combat the gambling industry or help individuals struggling with gambling addictions. Both your spending and giving are consistent with your internal values on gambling. However, a values-based investor would take it a step further and invest only in stocks or mutual funds that steer clear of the gaming industry. A values-based investor realizes the inconsistency of owning and profiting from gambling companies that oppose personal spending habits and giving decisions!

Griffin Johnson, a Christian radio talk show host, discovered the real-life application of this concept in his own investments recently. Griffin is passionate about his religious beliefs and seeks to incorporate these principles into every area of his life. This can be seen in his relationship to his children and wife, his outspoken views expressed through his radio program, and his involvement in church and other ministries.

However, when Griffin sat down with his financial advisor to review his retirement portfolio, he discovered that a portion of his mutual fund holdings were invested in corporations involved in such industries as pornography and abortion. He was outraged that he was profiting from the very industries that he often fought against in the public eye!

Griffin's situation, unfortunately, is not unique. The accumulation of assets in the form of equities has outpaced investors' ability to know exactly where their money is going and whose values it is supporting.

There has been tremendous growth in the capital markets over the last twenty years. The Dow Jones Industrial Average® now has risen above 11,000, primarily spurred on by the explosive growth of the mutual fund industry. Today there are over 10,000 mutual funds with over $5 trillion invested. Over 50 percent of

American households own shares of a mutual fund, either as a direct investment or as a part of their retirement plan. This phenomenon, although positive for many Americans, has created a wall of separation between you as a mutual fund owner and the types of companies you hold in your mutual fund portfolio.

When you invest your money in a mutual fund, it is combined with billions of other dollars invested by thousands of other shareholders. The mutual fund portfolio manager then uses this large pool of money to make stock purchases on behalf of the fund and you, the fund shareholder. The majority of portfolio managers only look at the financial considerations of the stocks they purchase; they don't think to consider the political, theological, or social dynamics of these companies.

This is an important consideration. Peter Drucker, one of the most well respected management gurus in American history, commented on this fact in a 1997 interview in *Forbes* magazine:

> The combined sources of money from retail investors, pension funds and retirement plans are the fastest-growing source of money (to the world economy). The most important source of capital is the average mutual fund transaction of $10,000.

Your money, combined with money of thousands of other investors, is an important source of capital for corporations. And that brings us to the key issue of this book: What kinds of companies are you supporting through your investments, and do they align with your personal values?

For example, *Playboy*, the largest and most well-known producer of pornography in the country, is traded on the New York Stock Exchange®. Walt Disney®, a stock included in the S&P 500®, has come under fire by many religious groups for apparent support of the homosexual lifestyle and the distribution of questionable films through their subsidiaries. American Express®, another S&P 500® company, promotes the homosexual agenda through corporate donations to homosexual activist groups and the sponsorship of gay and lesbian events.

These are the types of companies that mutual funds hold in their portfolios, thus making unsuspecting mutual fund shareholders direct owners of these companies and supporters of their values.

The exciting news is that today, thanks to new technology, your values and your money no longer need to be disassociated. Research and technology have combined to develop tools that will enable you to determine precisely where your money is invested and how it aligns with your values. A powerful example of this is the new Internet site, moneyandvalues.com, which has been launched recently to peer underneath the hood of your mutual fund portfolio to determine just how much of your current mutual fund is invested in companies that you may find objectionable. Using state-of-the-art technology (featured on the Discovery Channel's® "Technology Today" program), moneyandvalues.com utilizes the research of two of the values-based industry leaders, IRRC (http://www.irrc.org) and Values Investment Forum (http://www.valuesforum.com), to run an analysis of over 5,000 mutual funds and produce a customized report for each investor.

The process allows investors to choose from up to ten controversial issues that may be of personal concern to the investor, such as abortion, pornography, the environment, military contractors, nuclear power, etc., and create a Personal Values Profile. Investors then simply list any mutual funds that are personally held, such as those in an IRA or 401(k), any annuities or variable universal life insurance. The technology then compares the investor's Personal Values Profile (what your values are) with where investment dollars actually are placed (the values represented by your money).

Once you have determined exactly where you stand with regard to your values and your current investments, the site will make recommendations of alternative financial products that more closely match your personal values. moneyandvalues.com plans to offer this service to banks, credit unions, brokerage houses, and online trading firms. In the near future, it may be likely that no matter where you purchase your financial services, you will be asked, "Would you like your personal values reflected in your investment decisions?"

The development of the Internet and the access to information it gives investors is a very important step in the development of the values-based marketplace. As we saw in the example above with Griffin Johnson, a lack of knowledge about the issue of values-based investing keeps many well-intentioned people from taking action. However, with the introduction of web sites such as moneyandvalues.com, the information is becoming readily available to investors, both inexpensively and instantaneously through your modem.

The information is there. The key question is, "Are you going to use it to take action?"

Sir John Templeton, one of the greatest investors of the modern era and founder of the Templeton Funds, spoke clearly on the concept of values-based investing when he said:

> You wouldn't want to be the owner of a company that is producing harm for the public, and therefore, you wouldn't want to be the owner of a share of a company that's producing harm for the public.

Sir John practiced what he preached in the management of his own funds. Templeton Funds always have had a strong reputation for steering clear of problematic industries, such as tobacco, while building a successful financial track record.

Think of aligning your values with your financial decisions as a three-legged stool. The first leg is your charity. The second leg is your spending. And the final leg is your investing. When all three legs of the stool are aligned properly, you've got a sure foundation upon which to build a more fulfilling, purposeful, and impactful life that can transcend well beyond your mortality.

A History of Values-based Investing

How did values-based investing come about, and how long have individuals and institutions been practicing it? Although this analysis is not designed to be exhaustive, it will give you an overview of some of the important events in the life of this investment discipline. In addition, the process of aligning your values with your investments has been called many things: values-based investing, socially responsible investing, and ethical investing are three names generally used for the process. We will use these terms interchangeably in tracing the history of this movement.

Not surprisingly, the roots of values-based investing are grounded in religion. In biblical times, Jewish law directed individuals on how to invest their resources in a manner that reflected their ethical values. The laws laid out the processes for investing in land and the rules that were to govern these transactions to assure the ethical treatment of all parties involved.

In the 16th century, Quakers in the U.S. would not profit from the slave or war industries because of their beliefs on human equality and nonviolence. Their strong religious convictions helped shape their worldview on how men and women should be treated.

In 1928, the Pioneer Fund became the first socially responsible mutual fund. It was designed for evangelical Protestants who did not desire to profit from the alcohol or tobacco industries during the Age of Reform in America. Those religious investors who invested in the Pioneer Fund were the beginning of the values-based investing movement in the U.S.

The movement lay relatively dormant from the launching of the Pioneer Fund to the 1960s. Most values-based investors were motivated by the desire to align their values with their investments. Values-based investing was primarily a personal discipline designed to help people live out a consistent worldview based on their values.

The social climate of the 1960s raised concerns among some investors about civil rights and the military. Because activism was an important component of this politically and culturally volatile decade, many people began to consider the political ramifications of their investment decisions.

In 1965, church groups contracted Saul Alinsky to mobilize Rochester, New York's black community against Eastman Kodak®. Alinssky formed a coalition to improve living conditions and job opportunities for blacks in Rochester. In 1967, proxies were withheld for the first time at a shareholder meeting when they confronted Eastman Kodak's management at the company's annual meeting.

In 1970, Ralph Nader submitted nine General Motor®'s shareholder resolutions on minority hiring, representation on GM®'s board, and consumer rights. The Securities and Exchange Commission allowed two of the resolutions to appear on the ballot. This was significant because no one had ever placed values-based issues on a proxy ballot before. For the first time investors had the opportunity to use their money as a political tool to create corporate change based on their values.

In 1971, U.S. churches and religious orders formed the Interfaith Center on Corporate Responsibility (IRRC) to challenge corporate practices through shareholder resolutions. That same year, the Pax World Fund, founded by two Methodist ministers, was the first fund to screen for social issues such as war-related industries.

However, the turning point for socially responsible investing came during the campaign to eliminate the institutionalized racial discrimination of apartheid in South Africa. In 1971, the Episcopal Church petitioned GM® to divest its holdings in South Africa. Universities and public pension funds alike began to sell their stock in companies with operations in South Africa during the 1970s. In the 1980s, legislation was passed that negatively impacted corporations doing business in South Africa. This resulted in a massive outflow of capital and businesses in South Africa during the 1980s. The outcry of shareholder activists and the passing of penalizing U.S. legislation are believed to have been major contributors to the collapse of apartheid in the early 1990s.

Apartheid, more than any other issue, helped raise public awareness of the relationship between one's values and one's investments. Both institutions and individuals alike realized that values-based investing was not only a tool for aligning their values with their investments, but also a potent agent for corporate and political change. As a result, a plethora of financial products were launched in the 1980s and 1990s around the environment, tobacco, worker rights, and other relevant social issues.

CURRENT STATUS OF
VALUES-BASED INVESTING

Total investments using at least one social screen have grown from $40 billion in 1984, to $639 billion in 1995, to over $2 trillion today, according to a report by the Social Investment Forum (http://www.socialinvest.org). Social investments now account for about 13 percent of the estimated $16.3 trillion invested in mutual funds and professionally managed accounts in the U.S., according to the Social Investment Forum.

The number of socially responsible mutual funds using one or more social screens has grown from only a handful in the early 1970s to over 200 today. Almost every asset class is covered by socially responsible funds including equity, balanced, international, bond, index, and money market funds. Hundreds of institutional and mutual fund investors have used their rights as owners of public companies to file shareholder resolutions or vote their proxies on socially responsible issues.

Another interesting trend in the values-based movement is the launching of financial products and screening services designed to help bring values-based investing back to its evangelical roots of the 1920s. During the last five years, over thirty mutual funds have been formed around issues of concern to evangelical Christians. Research firms have been formed by evangelicals to address issues of concern not currently covered by socially responsible firms. These issues include abortion, pornography, and the relationship of corporate America to the homosexual political movement.

Many evangelical institutional investors are now beginning to incorporate these issues into their investment policies in an effort to live out their faith in their investment decisions. The Values Investment Forum (http://www.valuesforum.com) is playing a major role in this movement at the institutional level.

Wherever your values lie, there is a high probability that you should be able to find either a mutual fund or investment manager who will reflect your personal values in the investment management process. Today there is a national network of financial advisors, the Values Financial Network, who have been trained in the practice of values-based investing and who have the technology to assist you in developing an entire financial plan that reflects your personal values. The quality of managers, the financial return of screened mutual funds, and the growth of assets and products available make values-based investing a legitimate and achievable investing discipline.

So how can you implement a values-based strategy? We will take a look at the practical application of values-based investing in your portfolio in the next chapter.

Since the majority of values-based investing at the individual investor level is originated through the screening of personal stock or mutual funds portfolios, it may be helpful to consider the screens typically available to investors.

CHAPTER 2

Aligning Values with Investments

In the previous chapter, we discussed what values-based investing is all about. Now, let's turn our attention to the process of values screening and learn exactly how we can align our money with our personal values. There are three strategies that both individual and institutional investors use in the process of aligning their values with their investments.

SCREENING

The term "screening" is used to describe the process of choosing to include or exclude stocks from your portfolio based on your unique values. Investors typically exclude companies with products or practices that contradict their personal beliefs. This type of screening is called avoidance or "negative screening." Typical negative screens are alcohol, gaming, and tobacco.

Many investors have sought to invest in companies based on positive contributions to society. This type of screening tends to be more subjective and is called "positive screening." An example of positive screening would be companies that have a good track record regarding employee relations.

For the average individual investor, the research involved in formulating both positive and negative screening criteria can be overwhelming. Therefore, they tend to invest in values-based mutual funds with their screening criteria outlined in the fund's prospectus. A large percentage of the values-based mutual funds in the marketplace today are managed via a negative screening mandate, with the primary emphasis on avoiding certain violating industries.

Since institutional investors typically manage large pools of assets, they have the resources to customize the screening process by working with research and investment consultants. Many institutions construct a Social Policy Statement to guide their investment managers in the types of companies to avoid.

As with the retail marketplace, the majority of institutional investors employ a negative screening criteria. For example, a Catholic organization's social policy will state that their investment managers should avoid investing in corporations involved in the alcohol, gaming, tobacco, and abortion industries.

We will discuss the typical issues available for screening later in this chapter.

SHAREHOLDER ACTIVISM

The second avenue used to implement a values-based investment strategy is shareholder activism. When you own stock in a company, you have many rights and responsibilities as a shareholder. Although at times it may seem that your few shares have no direct impact on corporate behavior or practices, that still does not negate your responsibility to keep informed of the activities of "your company." A growing number of values-based investors are using their rights as company owners to speak out against practices by the company that go against their personal values, such as employee wages or corporate philanthropy.

When Ralph Nader introduced the nine corporate resolutions at General Motors in 1970, only two of the resolutions were actually allowed on the ballot. And even those two resolutions did not receive enough votes to cause immediate changes in the company. However, one fortunate outcome of these resolutions was that GM appointed the Reverend Leon Sullivan, an African American clergyman, to the auto maker's board. The next year, Sullivan demanded that GM withdraw from South Africa because of apartheid, and eventually collaborated with twelve other corporations to develop a statement of principles (known as the Sullivan Principles) for companies with business in South Africa. These principles were the first step of accountability for corporations doing business in South Africa and were a very important component of shareholders' success in ending apartheid.

Shareholder resolutions rarely pass. But as in the case of GM and apartheid, they often open the door for shareholder activists to dialogue with corporations on social issues. This dialogue can lead to a positive outcome.

For the most part, shareholder resolutions are submitted by institutional investors and mutual funds. The Interfaith Center on Corporate Responsibility has been a major leader in introducing shareholder resolutions dealing with social issues. On occasion, a well-informed individual investor will submit a resolution.

Many of the socially responsible mutual funds and investment advisory firms construct shareholder resolutions that align with the social goals outlined in their prospectus. This is why it is important to examine closely the issues that a socially responsible mutual fund includes in its screening. If you are not careful, you may find yourself investing in companies aligned against your values through your socially responsible mutual fund *and* the fund managers may be pressuring corporate change through shareholder resolutions in direct opposition to your values!

I remember discussing the concept of values-based investing with a potential chief financial officer candidate whom I was interviewing. As I talked, he looked at me with a rather cynical smile. When I paused, he said, "I already invest with my values. My primary investment is in the Washington Mutual Fund." Now, I knew this gentleman to be a strong evangelical Christian. I also knew that while the Washington Mutual Fund, in fact, had no holdings in the alcohol, tobacco, and gambling industries, the Fund was a substantial violator in the areas of abortion, pornography, and same-sex lifestyle—issues that he would consider to be of deleterious moral consequence. When I pointed this out to him, he was both amazed and frustrated.

COMMUNITY INVESTING

The third avenue used to implement a values-based investing strategy is through community investing. This initiative creates dollars for foundations and organizations that promote certain values. For example, the Values Financial Network, the "trade association" of financial advisors across the country who specialize in values-based investing, donates up to 10 percent of its revenue to a foundation. The foundation, through a donor advised fund, then directs grants to organizations such as Compassion International, Promise Keepers, Renaissance Foundation, and others based on the suggestions of its customers. Thus, whether the financial product sold through the VFN utilizes screening or not, it has an impact on the overall revenue of the VFN and, therefore, the financial contribution made to values-conscious organizations.

Another form of community investing mobilizes investment capital toward philanthropic goals. Certain forms of community investing place your capital with nonprofit lenders that build affordable homes, finance small businesses, and fund community development facilities like child care facilities.

This type of community investing is one of the most direct ways for values-based investors to put money into "grassroots" development programs while providing an adequate return on their investments. While community investing often provides only a modest return to investors, it helps people both in the U.S. and around the world who normally would be shut off from capital to create better lives through small loans. Often loans as small as $50.00 can have a dramatic impact on the borrower's life in poor countries.

ISSUES AVAILABLE FOR SCREENING

Since the majority of values-based investing at the individual investor level is originated through the screening of personal stock or mutual funds portfolios, it may be helpful to consider the screens typically available to investors.

Keep in mind as you consider the issue of screening that no company is perfect. Persons who have spent time thinking through the activities that go on daily at a company they own through their mutual fund should be able to think of at least one practice from which they would rather not profit. Since corporations are entities managed by individuals with different values and perspectives, you should not expect to find a company that manifests only your particular values in every specific way...it's just not possible.

This reality should not dissuade you, however, from seeking to implement screens in your investing process. There are many things in our lives that are not perfectly black and white. Yet that doesn't mean simply doing nothing and exclaiming, "Since it can't be done perfectly, I'm not going to try!"

One of my biggest frustrations in the financial market-place has been the ability of some financial leaders (who should be the most concerned about values) to use this point as an excuse to do nothing. These same leaders will extol the benefits of retirement planning or asset alloca-tion even though these processes also are impacted by outside variables that one cannot anticipate during the planning process. These disciplines, like investment screening, are not black and white; nonetheless, they are important dynamics of a successful, prudent investment plan and should be implemented despite their lack of certain guarantees.

A classic example of this is the attitude of a certain well-known Christian retirement planning firm. Although they regard themselves as the best in the retirement planning business for any and all Christian ministries and organizations, they refuse to consider values-based investing when constructing a retirement plan for a client. Instead, they turn a blatant blind eye to whose values are being supported with the hundreds of millions of retirement plan dollars created by these Christian ministries! I know for a fact that the abortion and pornography industries are well represented in the funds utilized by this Christian retirement planning service. How's that for values contradiction?

As an individual investor most likely investing in values-based mutual funds, your most important task is to decide which screens are most important to you. Don't expect to find a values-based mutual fund that perfectly aligns with all of your values in its screening...it's probably not out there.

Do examine the issues screened by a values-based fund to determine if the definitions of the screens match your beliefs. Be careful that you don't inadvertently compromise your values by being courted with vague terms such as "socially responsible." Who knows what the term "socially responsible" actually means. Like "family values," the term means one thing to a conservative and something entirely different to a moderate or liberal.

Although there are a plethora of screening issues and definitions in the marketplace, the following ten issues and their descriptions are some of the most common found in the values-based marketplace.

Negative Screens

- **Abortion**—This screen considers companies that manufacture or distribute abortion-causing drugs or contraceptives that can function as an abortion agent, hospitals that perform elective abortions, and/or healthcare plans that cover abortions. Other abortion issues considered include corporate contributions to organizations that perform or promote abortions and distributors of contraceptives that can function as an abortion-causing agent. If you are pro-choice, you may not want to apply this screen. If you are pro-life, this would be an important screen for you to consider.

- **Alcohol**—This screen considers alcohol producers and wholesale distributors.

- **Affirmative Action**—This screen considers companies that lack corporate board diversity and/or have recently been involved in major labor disputes. If you are a proponent of affirmative action, or are pro-union, you may want to apply this screen.

- **Defense Contracting**—This screen considers companies that are major defense contractors in the U.S., manufacture firearms or related ammunition products for nonmilitary markets, and/or derive revenue from the recent manufacture of nuclear weapons. If you are a pacifist, you would naturally want to apply this screen. If, on the other hand, you are a member of the

National Rifle Association, you probably would not want to apply this screen.

- **Environment**—This screen considers companies that have poor environmental records based on toxic emissions, oil and chemical spills, and/or fines.

- **Gambling**—This screen considers companies that operate casinos, lotteries, and/or manufacture commercial gaming equipment.

- **Nuclear Power**—This screen considers companies that own or operate nuclear power plants.

- **Pornography**—This screen considers companies that manufacture pornography in any format and/or operate adult cabarets. Other pornography issues that may cause a company to be excluded include pornography distribution, hosting pornographic web sites, profiting from the sale of pornographic banner ads, and advertising in pornographic magazines.

- **Same-Sex Lifestyles**—This screen considers companies with corporate activities that promote same-sex lifestyles. These activities include corporate contributions to gay and lesbian activist organizations, providing domestic partner benefits to employees, corporate sponsorship of pro-homosexual events, and/or advertisers in gay and lesbian magazines. If you consider the institutionalization of the same-sex lifestyle to be immoral, you would probably want to apply this screen. If, on the other hand, you were an advocate for same-sex lifestyle as an acceptable alternative, you probably would not want these companies excluded from your investments.

- **Tobacco**—This screen considers companies that grow, process, and/or manufacture tobacco products as well as companies that wholesale distribute tobacco products.

Other negative screens include animal testing, fair employment (whatever that may mean to an employee/employer), human rights, and labor relations. The ten listed above are the most common for numerous reasons, including the amount of quality research that exists on the issue, and the availability of financial products that reflect those issues.

Critics of negative screening often note that simply avoiding companies has no measurable impact on harmful corporate activities. They would note that for every person selling a company for social reasons there is someone on the other side of the transaction willing to own the company.

While there is some truth to the argument, many people implement negative screening simply as a personal decision to align their values with their investments. The process is beneficial for the person's own internal well-being. Also, it is interesting to note that when enough people agree on a negative screen, the cumulative effect of exclusionary screening for some combined with shareholder advocacy for others can make an overall impact on corporate behavior. The recent struggles of the tobacco industry are a good example of this.

POSITIVE SCREENING

Many investors are using positive screens to become more proactive in the values-based process. Under this system, the investor seeks to support companies that are positive models in the marketplace on issues of concern. For instance, companies producing environmentally friendly products or having strong track records in employee relations are often sought by positive screeners.

One of the main hurdles to positive screening is the element of subjectivity. Most negative screens tend be relatively black and white and can be implemented rather easily.

Positive screens require an analysis of very complex issues fraught with subjectivity. However, many within the socially responsible industry believe that the future of the industry rests in this methodology.

One of the most visible socially responsible research organizations is Kinder, Lydenberg and Domini (KLD). In formulating positive screening criteria, the following approach is taken by the firm:

We must apply a different methodology which we call the 'bellwether' approach. In the Middle Ages, shepherds simplified finding their flocks by putting a bell on the sheep—the bellwether—its companions followed. Find the bellwether and find the flock.

A similar principle applies in screening qualitative issues. Experience has shown that a combination of bellwether issues indicate companies' overall performance in a screening area. For instance, a company's relations with its unionized workers often reflects its record generally on employee and employment issues. Bellwethers are critical to effectively implementing qualitative social screens.

Certain standards stated as objectively as possible must stand for the company's performance generally. They help sort and organize a vast quantity of data. Thus, bellwethers are to the social side of investing what ratios, like the price/earnings ratio, are to the financial side.[1]

Positive screens tend to be much more subjective than the negative screens typically used in the mutual fund universe.

OTHER SCREENING METHODOLOGIES

As mentioned earlier, the Values Investment Forum (http://www.valuesforum.com) is a research firm whose focus is on screening issues of importance to Christian investors. The Forum has developed a hybrid screening methodology it calls Qualitative Rating System.

The Forum covers six negative screening issues: abortion, pornography, non-marriage lifestyles, alcohol, gaming, and tobacco. Under each of the broad issues, there are approximately thirty screening parameters. For example, the following are the parameters for the issue of abortion:

Manufacturer (3)	Develops/manufactures abortifacients
Hospital/Surgical Center	Performs elective abortions
Insurance (4)	Insures elective abortions
Contributor (5)	Gives to abortion activist groups
Distributor (6)	Distributes abortifacients

One of the difficulties in implementing negative screening is deciding where to draw the line. How far is enough? Also, doesn't it make sense that a manufacturer of an abortion-inducing drug should be held to a higher standard than a distributor of such drugs?

In response to this, the Forum assigns a numeric weighting to each parameter based on the firm's internal research on a particular issue and parameter. The higher the number, the more egregious the violation in the eyes of the Forum. Therefore, the abortion drug producer would be assigned a higher numeric value than the distributor of such a drug.

Once all of the parameters have been designed a numeric weighting, the Forum's technology then calculates a score for each company in its research database. Companies that score over a certain defined threshold are eliminated from investment consideration.

The value of this type of system to the socially conservative values investor is that all of the potential parameters of concern are included in the values screen. The system seeks to:

- Avoid companies that produce products that are aligned against biblical truths.

- Promote companies whose activities and products benefit humanity.

- Interact positively with companies that may commit activities prohibited in the Bible, but whose business practices and purposes are not primarily aligned against biblical truth in an effort to bring about positive corporate change.

---

[1]Peter Kinder, Steven D. Lyndenberg, Amy Domini, *Investing for Good* (Harper Collins Publishers, 1993), 62-63.

*What difference
does it make where one invests
his or her money
since the company actually
receives no direct benefit
from the investment?*

CHAPTER 3

Resources for the Values-based Investor

The Internet has made information on values-based investing available to the average investor at the click of a mouse. However, sometimes it may be difficult to find one place to obtain up-to-date information on socially responsible mutual funds, research, shareholder activism, and other values-based issues.

Following is a synopsis of several sites you may find useful in aligning your money with your values. You also will find a number of sites for values-based fund companies...where you'll often find very useful (although sometimes biased) information.

GENERAL VALUES-BASED SITES

Moneyandvalues.com—By far the most practical resource on the Internet for values-conscious investors is a new site, moneyandvalues.com. I say practical because although other sites offer information, http://www.moneyandvalues.com also offers you the opportunity to screen your existing investments on the spot and then consider alternatives that are recommended as closer correlatives to your personal values. Plans are to offer online trading, as well. moneyandvalues.com allows you to look under the hood of your mutual fund, variable annuity, or variable universal life investment to determine if your assets match your values. The site allows you to screen your investments using ten screening issues covering the entire political spectrum. So, whether you consider yourself socially conservative, liberal, or somewhere in between, this site has it all. Another interesting function of this site is that once you have listed the issues that are important to you, it will then examine certain values-based investments available in the marketplace and recommend alternatives that may match your specific values most closely.

Socialinvest.org—The site of the Social Investment Forum. SIF is a not-for-profit group that specializes in values-based investing. Here you will find great research on whether socially responsible investing negatively impacts returns (it doesn't!), how much money is currently being managed using social screens (a lot!), and other interesting facts on how to align your values with your investments. The site also provides a useful grid of the values-based funds currently available and what screening issues they use.

Socialfunds.com—Developed by SRI World Group, this is a values-based firm that provides information to retail investors. This site provides a most helpful chart outlining the performance of some of the universe of values-based mutual funds by investment objective. It also contains a number of practical tools, including limited individual stock research and a fund analyzer that screens funds on a number of values-based issues.

VALUES-BASED MUTUAL FUND COMPANY INTERNET SITES

Shepherdvalues.com—Shepherd Financial Services is the first company dedicated to offering multiple investment options (mutual funds, retirement plans, annuities, etc.) specifically for the socially conservative investor. The Shepherd Family of Mutual Funds screen out companies involved in abortion, pornography, gambling, alcohol, and tobacco by prospectus, as well as companies that violate certain same-sex lifestyle parameters. The Funds are aimed at the Christian/socially conservative investor and boast a lineup of well-known money managers including Nicholas-Applegate (small cap) and Templeton (international). SFS features a complete family of mutual funds covering most every asset class for the socially conservative investor.

Calvert.com—This slick site displays the fund offerings of one of the oldest values-based fund families, Calvert Social Investments. The site's "Know What You Own" program allows you to see how your fund stacks up using a few, limited screening criteria. The fund also has a link to the Calvert Foundation, an excellent source for information on community investing.

Domini.com—The Domini Social Equity Fund is one of the largest values-based index funds in the market-place and this site gives detailed information about its screening criteria. The site also publishes share-holder resolutions filed by the firm.

Citizensfunds.com—This site is one of the larger players in the values-based marketplace. One interesting feature of the site is that it lists each company in the Citizens Index and why the company passes Citizen's values-based screening criteria.

Mmapraxis.com—This web site is run by the Menonnite Mutual Aid, which gives updated statistics on the MMA Praxis funds and the firm's values screens.

Noahfund.com—This is the web site of the Christian fund known as the Noah Fund. The site lists the firm's screening criteria and philosophy on screen-ing as well as rates of return for the fund.

VALUES-BASED RESEARCH WEB SITES

Irrc.org—The Investor Responsibility Research Center is one of the oldest research firms focused on values-based issues. The IRRC operates an in-depth site that provides a volume of information primarily for the institutional investor. Moneyandvalues.com, the first site listed in this list, utilizes IRRC's research for the evaluation of mutual funds from a socially liberal perspective.

Valuesforum.com—The Values Investment Forum focuses its research on issues of concern to Christian investors: abortion, pornography, same-sex lifestyles are covered by the firm in addition to alcohol, gaming, and tobacco. The Forum works with many of the nation's most well-known religious organizations. Moneyandvalues.com utilizes the Forum's research to evaluate mutual funds from a socially conservative perspective. The Shepherd Values Funds listed earlier use research from VIF, as well.

Kld.com—KLD is the social research firm behind the Domini Social Equity Fund. Its research is primarily aimed at institutional investors and investment professionals.

FREQUENTLY ASKED QUESTIONS REGARDING VALUES-BASED INVESTING

When you buy a publicly traded stock, whether as part of your mutual fund or individually, your investment dollars are not actually being used by the company you're investing in. Your dollars are going to the seller of the stock through the exchange the stock trades on.

Therefore, what difference does it make where one invests his or her money since the company actually receives no direct benefit from the investment?

This statement is true technically; however, when you buy a stock, you are still an owner of that company. You get a certificate, have voting rights, and *most importantly, you profit based upon the activities of that company.* For example, when you own a drug stock that manufactures an abortion causing drug, then the more of that drug the company sells, the greater the profit that should be derived by the company. If you are pro-life then you must conclude that the more product sold equates to more babies dying as a result of the drug. As a result, the fact of the matter is that you will profit from the increase in revenues and profit (which results in the increased deaths of innocent children) through either stock appreciation or dividends.

Also, bring this thought down to a more personal level. Say that your next-door neighbor comes to your home one day with the following proposition. He owns private stock in a company in your city that has increased sales by 100% every year for the last five years and is generating huge profits for the shareholders. In addition, the value of his stock has increased every year by over 50%! Unfortunately, he is being forced to sell his shares because he is in a financial bind and is willing to sell you his shares at a substantial discount for your cash.

You're obviously interested at such a lucrative sounding investment. However, when you ask him the name of the company, he replies that it is the city's largest abortion clinic! If you are pro-life and true to your personal values, you politely will decline, regardless of the profit potential.

Under this scenario, had you purchased the stock your investment dollars would have gone to your neighbor, not the abortion clinic. The clinic would have not been impacted either positively or negatively by the transaction. Then why not do it? Because your strong personal beliefs against abortion would not have allowed you to be an owner of such a company. We believe this same principle holds true on the public exchanges as well. Principle and personal values, though quite different, should be an equal consideration to profit.

• • • • • •

I want to invest in a manner that is consistent with my beliefs, but where do you draw the line? It seems like all companies are involved in one way or the other in activities that I would oppose. And it's impossible to get accurate information on all 10,000 mutual funds. Why try?

Once again, there is some truth to the above concern. If you really think through what activities corporations are involved in and how corporations interrelate, it can be mind-boggling. The truth is that almost every publicly traded company may produce a product or be involved in an activity that you oppose.

However, in our opinion, there are some companies whose activities or products are so blatantly opposed to certain personal values that there should be no question that one should seriously consider these activities before making an investment in the company. For example, what about a company that produces hard-core pornography? What societal good does the product of this company produce? Who benefits from the manufacture of pornography? Does the user? Most would argue the user actually experiences personal moral decay. Then why should you own a piece of that company?

Where one draws the line is a personal choice. The point is each individual should make an *attempt to draw the line somewhere with the knowledge and information available to him or her at that time!* It is our belief that if more individuals attempted to draw this line, then more accurate information would become publicized and more choices available, which is good for everyone.

Research firms such as the Values Investment Forum and web sites such as moneyandvalues.com seek to provide the most accurate research at the point where you individually choose to draw that line.

• • • • • •

But even if I make a substantial purchase in a stock, I own so little of the company relative to the shares outstanding. What difference does it make in light of this?

Let's go back to the example of your neighbor who offers to sell you his stock in your city's largest abortion clinic. Does it make any difference whether he offers to sell you 50% of the company versus 1%? Or what if it was only one-tenth of 1% of the stock? Would you buy the stock then? Most pro-life individuals would not want to own any of the shares of this type of company. This principle applies in the public markets as well.

• • • • • •

I want to be a good steward of my money. An important component of stewardship is the return I make on my money. If I try and apply my convictions, I may be forced to sacrifice return, thus failing in my stewardship responsibilities.

We would strongly agree that one of the primary goals of investing your money is for a strong financial return. However, with the knowledge that we have available to date, we do not believe that it is necessary to sacrifice return in order to invest with one's convictions. See Chapter 4, "It Pays to Be a Values-based Investor" for a more complete explanation.

• • • • • •

If I want to try and create change within a corporation, why not boycott the company's products instead of not owning the stock?

We certainly have no objections to boycotting if you feel led. Boycotting has had a positive impact on many companies in the past. We don't see boycotting or values-based investing as competing choices. In fact, one may feel led to implement both. We also find that in many cases, it is easier to simply avoid the purchase of a company's stock versus not buying a company's products. Many large cap companies have so many subsidiaries and divisions it is impossible for most consumers not to utilize at least one of their products on a daily basis.

Additionally, whereas you may not have an acceptable alternative product to substitute for the one you propose to boycott, there most certainly would be multiple alternative investment options should you decide to forego owning a particular company's stock.

• • • • • •

If my goal is to create positive change within a company, shouldn't I own the company's stock and try to work from within through shareholder activism to bring about the changes I desire?

This is a very legitimate point if your primary motivation is to create corporate change. Many institutional investors will own stocks in order to affect positive change. And they have had success. If your primary motivation for owning a stock is to create positive change, then we would encourage you to follow through on your rights as a shareholder to bring about that change. Vote proxies, introduce shareholder resolutions, write company officers and express your opinions.

Most individual investors do not own a stock primarily to create positive change from within simply because these investors have no idea of what types of activities their stocks are involved in. Many people also have strong convictions that one should not own these corporations for any reason (see the first question). We can respect both viewpoints. If you choose this course of action to manifest your personal values with your investment dollars, be careful that you follow through and not use this tack simply as a cop-out. Done correctly, creating corporate change from within is an enormously time consuming task.

• • • • • •

I've seen Internet services that will evaluate your mutual funds using values screens and then recommend nonscreened funds as alternative investments? Will this work?

We believe the value of these types of services lies primarily as an education tool. Most investors simply do not know what types of companies they hold in their mutual fund portfolios. These types of services are great for peeling back the lid from your mutual fund and letting you determine if your investments match your values.

However, if you're looking to consistently align your values with your investments, we would not recommend buying a nonscreened fund simply because it may be invested in stocks that don't violate your values at a particular time. Why?

- **No values mandate by the fund**—A nonvalues-based fund has no prospectus mandate to follow social screens. The manager can buy whatever companies he or she feels will provide the best return. To do anything else would be a serious violation of the manager's fiduciary responsibility. Therefore, you can never be sure exactly what you will or will not own in the fund.

- **Turnover**—A nonscreened fund that looks clean today may not be clean tomorrow because of the lack of values screens. Many funds turn their whole portfolio over more than two times per year. Without a values screen, what is clean today may be rotten tomorrow.

- **Outdated Information**—Any type of evaluation of your mutual fund based on holdings is a snapshot of your portfolio holdings on one specific day in time. The evaluations can never be entirely accurate because of this.

If you want to determine just what type of companies you currently own in your mutual fund portfolio, log on to moneyandvalues.com. Not only will it give you an overview of where you currently stand in regards to your personal values in your portfolio, it also will recommend values-based products that align more closely with your values.

Section II

Values-based
Investment Management

Twelve of the seventeen values-based funds with assets more than $100 million received top rankings from either Lipper or Morningstar, or both.

CHAPTER 4

It Pays to Be a
Values-based Investor

One of the most interesting questions concerning values-based investing is, "Can you be a values-based investor and make money at the same time?" In other words, is it possible to invest for both social and financial return? As mentioned previously, this is the goal of the values-based investor: to achieve the double bottom line with one's investment dollars.

For years, the financial press for the most part considered values-based investing somewhat of an aberration. The perception was that those who espoused values-based investing were part of a small, idealistic, "do-gooder" community. The thought was that when the rubber really hit the road for the average investor, return was the most significant factor in the investment process, and values ranked somewhere way down the list.

You often would see financial publications make absurd claims about the effects of screening on an investment. I remember one such story boldly stating, "You can expect to earn around 3% per year less on a socially responsible mutual fund versus an unscreened one."

When I looked for the research statistics backing up this claim, none were listed. I then examined the qualifications of the author and determined that he was a freelance writer with only limited knowledge of the financial markets.

It is also amazing to hear the quotes of financial advisors who do not practice values-based investing in their own practice, but are portrayed as experts on the subject by the press. For example, one recent article on values-based investing had a quote by a Christian financial advisor who stated with authority, "Christian mutual funds tend to yield low rates of return." However, the top performing values-based mutual fund in 1998 was the Noah Fund, a fund marketed to Christians with conservative screening criteria. Since its inception, the fund has beaten the S&P 500® by almost 6% per year over the last three years. That sure doesn't seem like a "low return" that an investor is forced to live with for the sake of personal values.

Similarly, the Shepherd Values Funds entered the market in 1999 with well-known subadvisors such as Templeton Portfolio Advisors, Nicholas Applegate Capital Management and Cornerstone Capital. I can tell you with certainty that if those professional management firms thought that their performance would suffer as a result of managing a "values-screened fund" they would never enter into a subadvisory agreement in the first place.

So who are you to believe concerning the return on values-based investments? The answer can be found in looking at performance statistics on values-based mutual funds, research studies focused on values-based returns and, quite frankly, using a little common sense.

CASE #1: THE FINANCIAL RETURN OF VALUES-BASED MUTUAL FUNDS

One of the most recent studies on whether values-based investing pays was released by the Social Investment Forum in July 2000. Much of the information given below is taken directly from the Forum's web site. To get a more detailed description of this study, go to http://www.socialinvest.org.

The Forum analyzed the performance of socially responsible mutual funds through mid-2000 using Morningstar, Lipper Analytical Services, and Wiesenberge—three of the most trusted investment rating services in the business. The key findings of the Forum's analysis were as follows:

- **Over 70% of the largest socially responsible funds got top ratings by the three services.**

Twelve of the seventeen values-based funds with assets more than $100 million received top rankings from either Lipper or Morningstar, or both. Ten earned an "A" or "B" ranking from Lipper, based on one- and/or three-year total returns in their investment categories. Six received either four- or five-star ratings from Morningstar.

- **Over half of the larger universe of social funds—large and small—earned highest ratings by the ranking services.**

Of the forty-six funds with a three-year performance record tracked by the Forum, over 63% (twenty-nine) received the highest marks from either Lipper or Morningstar. The Forum states that nineteen of the funds received either an "A" or "B" ranking from Lipper based on one- and/or three-year total return within their investment categories. A total of nineteen funds garnered either four or five stars from Morningstar for three-year risk-adjusted return.

- **Top-performing socially screened funds exist in most major asset classes.**

The study showed that whether investors are looking for domestic equity, global, international balanced or bond investments, there's a competitive socially screened fund available to help them achieve their financial goals.

- **Of the sixty-five values-based mutual funds tracked by Morningstar, 11% (seven) received the firm's**

coveted five-star rating and 26% (seventeen) snared a four-star rating.

Only 10 percent of mutual funds in the broader Morningstar universe earn a five-star rating, and just 22 percent are awarded a four-star rating. In other words, at the time this study was conducted, you had a greater percentage chance of owning a four- or five-star rated mutual fund by Morningstar if your fund was values screened!

Another important trend pointed out in the study was that an increasing number of screened mutual funds offer investors greater opportunities to encourage higher levels of corporate social responsibility through shareholder action and community development investing. Not only does it reward you in the pocketbook to invest with your values, it also can help better your world.

Forum director/spokesperson Steve Schueth observed:

> The numbers don't lie. The underperformance myth has been busted. Even during a period of serious market volatility, on average socially screened funds of all types continue to equal or exceed the performance of non-screened funds. Even better, this excellent performance accompanies advocacy and community investing through their mutual funds.

Case #2: The Domini Social Index and the Good Money Averages

Domini Social Index

As mentioned earlier, the research firm of Kinder, Lydenberg and Domini (KLD) has done a tremendous job conducting socially responsible research and advancing the values-based investing movement. Early in the formation of their firm, they recognized the need for a credible socially responsible index that values-based investors could use as a benchmark for their portfolios.

So in 1988, they began to work on what would become one of the most recognized indexes in the socially responsible marketplace: the Domini Social Index. The following passage from their book *Investing for Good* explains the methodology behind the index formation:

> Our first task was to identify the nonfinancial screens socially responsible investors imposed. Then we had to develop a universe that passed them. This process was more difficult than it sounds. Some social investors apply only one or two screens, not the ten we use.
>
> We divided our screens into 'exclusionary' and 'qualitative' screens. Exclusionary screens came first historically and are the

first screens we apply. They are also negative in that they eliminate companies involved in business or activities that most social investors find unacceptable. Qualitative screens track corporate responses to the demands of today's society. It is in these areas that the future of socially responsible investing lies. They are positive screens. They demand evaluations of what a company is doing to make society better.

With the screens in place, choosing companies for the Domini Social Index (DSI) began. We conducted the selection process in three stages. In the first, we applied our screens to the S&P 500®; about 255 companies (51%) passed. We then turned to small capitalization companies, like Ben and Jerry's Homemade® and Isco® whose social stories—and good financial performance—made them essential to a social index. There were about forty-five of these.

Finally, we looked at companies not in the S&P 500® that were in the top 1,000 in terms of market capitalization and that were in the business sectors in which the Index was underrepresented. Of these, we kept about 100. It took twenty-six months to look at 1,000 companies, evaluate 800, and choose the 400 with which to construct a sufficiently diversified, large cap portfolio.[1]

The Domini Social Index was launched on May 1, 1990. Since that time, the DSI has outperformed the S&P 500® on a total return basis and on a risk-adjusted basis since its inception.

	1-Year	3-Year	5-Year	10-Year
Domini 400®	13.40%	22.49%	25.60%	21.35%
S&P 500®	16.36%	20.73%	24.06%	19.59%

Performance of the Domini Social Index as of August 31, 2000

One can see from this chart, that the Domini Social Index has outperformed that S&P 500® by almost 2 percent annually over the last ten years. Once again, further evidence for our case that values-based investing can make money while doing good.

The Domini Social Equity Fund was created by the firm to model the index. It also has outperformed the S&P 500® over the last five years. For more information, go to the fund web site at http://www.domini.com.

It is important to point out that given the tremendous political diversity that exists in the world of values-based investing, the Domini Social Index is not going to appeal to all socially responsible investors. After all, values are personal, and in some cases, exclusive. One is, for example, either pro-choice on abortion or pro-life. Investing in a way that reflects that personal value is what socially responsible, or values-based investing is all about. Any social index, or socially responsible mutual fund will, by definition, offer a specific and subjective set of values that it screens for. Whether a particular index or fund is consistent with your personal values can only be determined by examining its screening criteria.

GOOD MONEY AVERAGES

These were actually the first socially screened indexes launched in 1976 by Professor Ritchie Lowry of Boston College. Professor Lowery realized that socially responsible investing needed a legitimate way to respond to the myth of underperformance of screened investments. Professor Lowery designed two indexes to be compared against the Dow Jones Industrial and Utilities Averages.

The Good Money Industrial Average (GMIA) consists of thirty industrial companies favored by certain social investors. Since 1976, no companies in the index have been replaced because of performance. Replacements are made only because the company goes private, the company is merged with another company that is not socially responsible (based on their definition of "social responsibility"), or the company goes bankrupt. Also, a company may be removed from the GMIA if it "stubs its toe" on social issues.

The Good Money Utilities Average (GMUA) consists of fifteen utility companies and is comparable to the Dow Jones Utility Average.

The Good Money Industrial Average has a 2,045% cumulative return from 1976 to 1999. The return of the Dow Jones Industrial Average over this same period was 1,044%. This is an annualized increase of 29.1% for the GMIA versus 17.5% for the DJIA.

The Good Money Utility Average has a cumulative total return of 358% from 1976-1999. The return of the Dow Jones Utility Average over the same period was 161%. This is an annualized increase of 15.5% for the GMUA versus 11.8% for the DJUA.

RESEARCH STUDIES ON VALUES-BASED INVESTING

One impressive study on the impact of social investing on performance was conducted by John B. Guerard, Jr. in 1996. Mr. Guerard, who has been on Wall Street for ten years, is known to some industry professionals as a "scholar of Wall Street" and a leading thinker in investment theory, according to the Social Investment Forum. He holds an A.B. in Economics from Duke University and a Ph.D. in Finance from the University of Texas.

Mr. Geraurd's study found that returns in socially screened and unscreened universes do not differ significantly. His conclusion was that one should be careful when selecting a socially screened manager or mutual fund since performance can vary dramatically across managers, but should not vary due to social screening over the long term. For more on the Geraurd study, go to http://www.socialinvest.org.

COMMON SENSE

The Social Investment Forum released a study in 1999 entitled "1999 Report on Socially Responsible Investing Trends in the United States." One of the interesting trends noted in this study was that the assets in values-screened separate accounts grew by an impressive 210 percent from 1997 to 1999. These screened portfolios grew from $433 billion in 1997 to $1,343 billion in 1999. This number represents 89 percent of the total assets in screened portfolios (including mutual funds) at the end of 1999.

Separate accounts are individually managed accounts designed for high-net worth investors and institutions. Most larger institutions use individual accounts because of the ability to customize the account and the lower fees versus mutual funds.

Although we don't know the exact percentage, it would be a fair guess to say that a large portion of the assets held in screened separate accounts in America today are for institutional clients—such as religious institutions, colleges and universities, etc. These types of institutions have a high fiduciary responsibility in the management of the assets on behalf of the institution. They have vast resources to hire consultants and full-time staff members to oversee the funds. They have the assets to cherry-pick the finest money managers in the country. They screen their portfolios according to their social values. According to the study, 88 percent of managers for screened portfolios report using three or more screens in the management process.

It would make common sense that if these institutions—with their high fiduciary responsibilities and vast resources, screen their assets for social reasons—then it would follow that performance must not be hampered significantly.

There is one other interesting point to consider concerning the performance question. The Department of Labor issued a letter in May 1998 stating that investments, such as socially screened mutual funds, could be included in a retirement plan as long as the fiduciary determines that the mutual fund is expected to provide an investment return similar to alternative investments having similar risk characteristics.

Since this ruling, values-based mutual funds have reported phenomenal growth in the retirement plan marketplace because trustees feel comfortable that the investment performance of many values-based mutual funds will equal those of their unscreened counterparts.

Our belief is that, like any investment discipline, making money using values screens rests on one's ability to choose quality money managers with proven track records and pay reasonable fees for their services. Over the long-haul, we believe screening should have no dramatic impact—one way or the other—on an investor's return.

So, it is fair to say that values-based investors can invest for both financial and moral return. Implementing social screens does not mean you have to give up your retirement. As a matter of fact, you may even rest better during your retirement years knowing that your money produced a comfortable nest egg *and* a better world at the same time.

---

[1]Peter Kinder, Steven D. Lyndenberg, Amy Domini, *Investing for Good* (Harper Collins Publishers, 1993), 28-31.

Values-based managers tend to hold a strong belief in capitalism and the positive results of the system while realistically attempting to create positive corporate change in areas of concern.

CHAPTER 5

The Investment
Management Process

A s has been discussed in previous chapters, there has been an explosion recently in the amount of investment assets currently being managed using some type of social screens. Recently Vanguard, one of the largest mutual fund companies in the world, announced the formation of a values-based index fund that seeks to mimic the Calvert Social Index. Some of the top investment managers in the country are beginning to realize that values-based investing makes sense...and there is a real business opportunity for investment managers who offer products designed for values-based investors.

So how does an investment manager go about the process of utilizing values-based screens in the invest-ment management process? This chapter will attempt to address this question in an understandable and concise manner. Please realize that there are thousands of invest-ment managers in the marketplace and each one has his or her own processes that are unique for that particular manager. Therefore, this chapter will give only an overview of a typical values-based management process and may not apply to every values-based manager.

When you hire an investment manager, it is because you have confidence that this manager will perform well for you from a financial perspective. The ultimate goal of investing is to achieve financial return...it is why you put your capital at risk. Therefore, an investment manager's primary concern is on the financial return of a portfolio based on your desired level of risk. However, as one well-known values-based money manager in Boston recently stated, a manager who utilizes social screens in a portfolio is really "serving two masters," seeking to achieve superior financial and social return.

Oftentimes, there will be a tension between the financial and social interests in a portfolio. Choices must be made on issues that are sometimes gray in nature. And these choices can impact the financial return of the portfolio. However, as quality research and processes are developed, these choices can be made with accurate and timely information.

Jason Huntley, investment manager at Cornerstone Capital Management in Colorado Springs, Colorado, recently outlined his firm's investment management process and how they incorporate screens into their portfolios. Cornerstone's primary product is individual stock accounts managed for high-net worth and institutional clients with values screens.

Huntley states that from an investment management perspective, the values-based component comes as the very last step before you officially build the portfolio. Managers will implement financial screens to assemble a pool of stocks or bonds that they feel are the strongest from a potential performance basis.

After the financial screens are applied, there may be a pool of fifty investments that a manager feels are strong and timely. The portfolio manager will then take the client's specific values screens and eliminate companies that fail those screens. The remaining companies are used to construct a portfolio consistent with the client's financial and social objectives.

Huntley states that managers still are able to utilize their best stock ideas for a portfolio, but they eliminate stocks that violate the client's values. Huntley's experience has been that even when the client utilizes relatively strict screens, only five out of fifty stocks typically will be eliminated from consideration for a portfolio. This remaining number is adequate to build a diversified portfolio, according to Huntley.

This process is important because historically (very early on in socially responsible investment management), a manager would restrict the investable universe of stocks by first applying the values screens before the financial screens. The companies remaining after the values screen may have had great social records, but financial characteristics were not even considered up to this point. This limited the number of companies to invest in based on financial screens because the manager was left with a very limited universe of companies to choose among.

Because of this early screening process, portfolios would sometimes be so restricted that performance was affected negatively, leading to underperformance in a values portfolio. This may have contributed to the underperformance myth that has existed in the past concerning values-based investing.

Huntley believes that the tide in the investment management process turned around in 1996. The popularity of values-based investing started to increase as mutual fund companies like Dreyfus began creating mutual funds. More credible money managers entered the marketplace using social screens for their clients.

"The entire issue of performance, screened or not screened, still lies in manager talent. How has that manager incorporated values based criteria into their investment manage process? If not done adequately, the performance could suffer. What it boils down to is the talent of the manager, not the social screen," says Huntley in addressing this issue.

"Most of our clients never look at the screening as a performance damper because we educate them on the front-end. If we do underperform, we did not do the right job building the portfolio on the front-end," states Huntley.

Cornerstone's investment management style is a core process. This means that in working with an institutional client, Cornerstone typically manages the largest portion of a diversified portfolio since their management expertise lies in large companies with well-known names —the "cornerstone" of an institutional client's portfolio.

"We are a core manager because of values-based investing. Clients want the values component of their portfolio to be a central theme. They normally don't desire to be clean with only ten percent of their portfolio, they want the majority of it managed according to their values," reveals Huntley.

"Since most investors allocate the largest portion of their portfolio to large, brand-name companies, the bread and butter of their portfolio, we have focused on applying values-based screens to this portion of their portfolio," Huntley continues.

He further states that the education process with investors from a values-based perspective is much easier when talking about large companies like Coca-Cola® or IBM®. People know and trust these brands.

CORNERSTONE'S CORE PROCESS

Step One: Quantitative Analysis—the process of taking 13,000 companies and applying fundamental filters such as price to earnings (PE), return on equity, growth rates, and cash flow. The goal of this first process is to filter an unmanageable universe down to a workable universe of 200 to 300 companies.

Step Two: Sector Analysis—out of the 300 companies remaining, where should the managers now be looking for opportunities? This process involves economic and broad market factors and technical analysis on sectors.

Step Three: Fundamental Analysis—in which business models do the managers believe? What businesses do they want to own and at what price range do they want to own them? Cornerstone managers typically look for leaders or emerging leaders in industries.

Step Four: Assemble the Recommended List—these are stocks that the firm can buy for its clients immediately. The list typically consists of around forty to fifty companies. The managers then do more technical analysis to determine if it is the right time to buy a stock. Based upon this analysis, they can either under or over weight a position.

Step Five: Values-based Objectives—the managers then take into account the client's specific financial and values objectives. Normally, the values screens do not eliminate enough companies to increase risk in the portfolio since Cornerstone diversifies among industry sectors with the remaining names. The managers also do not make major bets on individual companies and seek to maintain blended portfolios.

As stated earlier, this process allows managers such as Cornerstone to pick from among the best stocks from a financial perspective for their clients' portfolios.

There is another benefit for both the investment manager and their clients when using values-based screens. Huntley states, "People are latching onto the philosophy behind values-based investing. It simply does not make sense for an individual concerned about the environment to invest in companies with poor environmental records. The values-based proposition opens up a whole new world of possibilities for a client. We tend to form the best relationships with our values-based investors."

If you would like to discuss the values-based process in greater detail, you may contact Jason Huntley at 800-939-4339, or visit their web site at http://www.ccmadvisers.com.

A COMMON MISCONCEPTION: INVESTMENT UNIVERSE

One common theme expressed by values-based managers is that there is a misconception by the investing public that once you apply social screens to a portfolio, your investment universe becomes too limited to manage effectively. This simply is not true.

One values-based manager overseeing $300 million in funds for a variety of institutional clients stated that the values screens employed by her firm eliminated only 2 percent of the S&P 500®, although some industries may be eliminated due to poor performance by industry participants as a whole. For example, Philip Morris only represents seventy-one basis points of the S&P 500®.

This firm used both positive and negative screening criteria in the process. This manager stated that in her opinion, there is no greater risk to the client because of social screening. Her portfolio has consistently outperformed the S&P 500® since inception.

PASSION FOR CORPORATE CHANGE

Many values-based managers who seriously work in the field exhibit a passion for creating positive corporate change utilizing values investing. They tend to hold a strong belief in capitalism and the positive results of the system while realistically attempting to create positive corporate change in areas of concern.

"There are finite environmental resources but capitalism often operates on the principle of unlimited environmental resources," says an experienced values manager. "Companies should be held accountable for their environmental records. Shareholders can assist in this process by voting proxies and introducing shareholder resolutions."

The values-manager further adds, "There are certain standards that should govern how companies interact with their employees. Sweatshops and labor camps violate human decency. Corporate shareholders can help make a positive difference if they will only stand up for common decency at the corporate level."

SHORT-TERM COSTS FOR LONG-TERM GAIN

Many values managers believe that even if there was a short-term cost for investing with your values, the long-term gains will far outpace the short-term cost.

"I believe that environmental-friendly companies will be rewarded financially in the long-run because of lessened liabilities associated with poor environmental practices," says one values manager.

"I believe that companies that take care of their employees and produce quality products that help mankind will profit in the long-run because of these actions. I believe that it is simply a matter of common sense and patience on behalf of the investor," says Patrick Johnson, president of the Values Investment Forum.

It only takes a bit of common sense to see the logic of this argument. And the good news is that because the values-based investment management process is a solid one, you may be able to profit in both the short and long run by aligning your values with your investments.

The man or woman
who stands up for his or her
convictions in the face of a
world that displays complete
apathy is truly a hero
in our culture today.

Values-based Investing—Who Cares?

A s we've seen in previous chapters, values-based investing is a conscious decision to align your investment assets with your deeply held personal values. It's about living out a holistic worldview in every part of your life.

The personal benefit of living out your convictions in every part of your life is peace of mind. It has been said that some of the most miserable people in life are those who know the truth, yet don't live it. Values-based investors seek to live out the truth and benefit dramatically from this effort.

Therefore, when addressing the question "Who cares about values-based investing?", it is important to remember that if not one person besides you actually cares, it really doesn't matter! The man or woman who stands up for his or her convictions in the face of a world that displays complete apathy is truly a hero in our culture today. The spiritual and emotional benefits of values-based investing (along with the financial return addressed earlier) make the process valuable if you were the only person doing it.

But as we will examine in this chapter, you are not the only person who cares. In fact, values-based investing is one of the fastest growing segments of the investing industry. There are now more values-based mutual funds and quality investment managers than ever before. Individual investors across the globe are beginning to see the impact that their investments can make when they are aligned with their values.

So not only are you *not* swimming against the current when you invest your money with your values, you are joining a virtual "Niagara Falls" of other investors who are practicing this discipline!

Lest you think my zeal for values-based investing is clouding my good judgement, I invite you to examine a number of the statistics in the marketplace that support the case for values investing.

THE SOCIAL INVESTMENT FORUM 1999 REPORT ON SOCIALLY RESPONSIBLE INVESTING TRENDS IN THE UNITED STATES

On November 4, 1999, the Social Investment Forum released this study documenting the explosive growth in the socially responsible industry. If you would like to read this report in greater detail, please go to the

Forum's web site at http://www.socialinvest.org. Below are a few of the research statistics on values-based investing released by the Forum as quoted in this report:

- Assets under management in a socially and environmentally responsible manner topped the $2 trillion mark in 1999. Social investments grew from $1.185 trillion in 1997 to $2.16 trillion in 1999.

- One out of every eight dollars under professional management in the United States today is part of a socially responsible portfolio. The $2.16 trillion being managed by major investing institutions (including pension funds, mutual fund families, foundations, religious organizations and community development financial institutions) accounts for roughly 13% of the total $16.3 trillion in investment assets under management in the U.S., according to the *1999 Nelson's Directory of Investment Managers*. That's up from 9% of the total in 1997.

- Growth of assets involved in ethical investment significantly outpaced the broad market. Socially responsible investing grew at twice the rate of all assets under professional management in the United States.

- Between 1997 and 1999, total assets involved in socially responsible investment grew 82%—from $1.185 trillion to $2.16 trillion. In the same period, according to a comparison of total assets under professional management in the United States reported annually in *Nelson's Directory of Investment Managers*, the broad market grew 42% (including both market appreciation and net cash inflows).

By socially responsible investment, the authors of this report mean assets involved in screening, shareholder advocacy or community development—the three primary tools of values-based investors.

Socially screened portfolios continued their explosive growth. Since 1997, total assets under management in screened portfolios for socially concerned investors rose 183%, from $529 billion to $1,497 billion. Assets in socially screened mutual funds grew by 60% to $154 billion, and assets in screened separate accounts grew 210%, to $1,343 billion.

- Nearly a trillion dollars is controlled by investors who play an active role in shareholder advocacy on social responsibility issues. Over 120 institutions and mutual fund families have leveraged assets valued at $922 billion in the form of shareholder resolutions. These institutional investors use the power of their ownership positions in corporate America to sponsor or cosponsor proxy resolutions on social issues.

- The fastest growing component of socially responsible investing is the growth of portfolios that employ both screening and shareholder advocacy. Assets in portfolios using both strategies grew 215%, from $84 billion in 1997 to $265 billion in 1999.

- Community investing grew by 35%. Assets held and invested locally by community development institutions totaled $5.4 billion, up from $4 billion in 1997.

The report states, "The Social Investment Forum's research finds that socially responsible investments are growing rapidly, providing competitive performance for investors, encouraging corporate responsibility and meeting needs in economically distressed communities."

EXPLOSIVE GROWTH OF VALUES-BASED MUTUAL FUNDS

As more and more investors begin to see the value of aligning their beliefs with their investments, there has been explosive growth both in the number and amount of assets managed by values-based mutual funds.

In the same report referenced above, the Social Investment Forum listed the growth of mutual funds using some type of social screening:

Screened Mutual Funds			
	1995	1997	1999
# of Funds	55	139	175
Assets*	12	96	154
*in billions			

Today, there are 200-plus mutual funds using some type of values screening in their investment management process. One of the interesting developments has come recently in the index arena, demonstrating the viability of values-based investing.

The two dominant socially responsible index funds in the marketplace today are the Domini Social Equity Fund ($1.4 billion) and the Citizen's Index ($717 million). Because of the success of these funds, and the overall growth of the values-based movement, two financial powerhouses have recently entered the market-place to capture a segment of this hot market.

The Vanguard Calvert Index Fund is a collaboration between two industry heavyweights: Vanguard Mutual Funds (one of the largest fund families in the world focusing on indexing), and Calvert (one of the largest fund families in the world focusing on socially responsible investing). This fund's benchmark index will exclude alcohol, tobacco, gaming and nuclear-power companies while including companies with such qualities as sound environmental records.

TIAA-CREF Social Choice Equity Mutual Fund was recently made available to retail investors. This fund is a product of the largest pension fund organization in the U.S., TIAA-CREF, with almost $300 billion in assets. Pension members have been investing in this fund already for ten-plus years.

Names like Vanguard and TIAA-CREF only help quicken the advance of values-based investing into mainstream American investing.

WHY MORE PEOPLE ARE INVESTING ACCORDING TO THEIR VALUES

As seen from both the dollar amounts invested and the number of values funds launched, values investing is on a fast-paced track. But why? Why are more investors seeing the light?

The Social Investment Forum's "1999 Report on Socially Responsible Investing Trends in the United States" gives three primary reasons for this explosive growth:

1. **Performance**—As previously discussed, there has been a performance myth associated with investing according to your values. This myth has kept many well-intentioned investors out of the values market-place. As more studies are released on the above-average performance of socially responsible mutual funds, many investors are beginning to see that they can do good both financially and socially by invest-ing in screened investments.

2. **Tobacco**—The growing anti-tobacco sentiment has motivated many investors to examine whether their mutual funds hold tobacco companies. Since these stocks are household names, an investor can easily

determine whether his or her mutual fund holds companies involved in this industry. Many institutions with billions under management are excluding tobacco companies.

3. **Retirement Plan Participation**—Employers are beginning to offer values-based funds to their employees through the company's retirement plans. In fact, the explosion of the growth of assets at many well-known, socially responsible firms has been driven by monies flowing in through corporate retirement plans.

So, if you are a values-based investor, you are not alone. There are hundreds of mutual funds and billions of dollars being managed according to values. As the performance myth has been disproven, and more retirement plans have begun offering values products, more Americans have jumped at these opportunities.

If you're not a values investor, what are you waiting for? Values investing is a case where "joining the crowd" is a good thing—both for your pocketbook and society.

*By far the greatest
number of investment options
available by product
category for
values-based investing
is mutual funds.*

CHAPTER 7

Values-based
Investment Options

T he development of values-based insurance and
investments is still, to a degree, in its infancy.
However, considerable progress is being made
that will forever change the financial services industry.
Following is an example of how what appeared to be an
insurmountable problem turned out to be the genesis for
a whole new way of creating values-based investments.

In late 1999, I was consulting with one of the largest
financial services companies in the world about how we
might introduce values-based investing to their product
line. At the time, I was the CEO of Shepherd Financial
Services, Inc., which had introduced a family of funds
designed specifically for the socially conservative
investor.

My intent was to get this enormous insurance
company to include Shepherd portfolios as an investment option in their variable annuity. However, doing so
would be a long, difficult process with no assurance of
success. For starters, the administrative and operations

issues are enormous. Then there are the ubiquitous regulatory issues. Then there are the political issues. If Shepherd funds were added as an investment option to appease the socially conservative investor, the insurance company might also feel compelled to add funds that catered to the socially liberal investor. The process has many angles and dynamics that make it daunting.

"I think what you have to do, Stephen, is find a way to separate the values proposition from the investment," admonished Gerry Weaver, Chief Marketing Officer.

I sat in my study, phone in hand, considering this unlikely proposition. "What?" I asked. "What are you talking about? How do you separate values from the product? That's impossible!"

Mutual funds are categorized either as "values-based" or not solely based on whether the fund screens for certain issues such as the environment, pornography, or tobacco. Most funds don't use any type of screening mechanism. Those funds that do screen, then, are considered "values-based."

Now, I enjoy abstract thinking. My intellectual recreation includes reading theological treatises, commentaries on political and philosophical thought, and business theory. Heck, my favorite author is Ayn Rand and her volumes on objectivist epistemology. But even for me, the thought of even attempting to separate "values" from mutual funds and still end up with a "values-based" investment was way out there.

In the days ahead, every time I considered Gerry's suggestion I would cringe as though I were suffering through the awful screech of someone's fingernails going across a blackboard.

However, with focus and time, we were able, in fact, to do what Gerry suggested. I think that it was Calvin Coolidge who said that no problem is so great that it can withstand the advantage of focused brainpower (paraphrase).

In the end, what resulted is today an exciting innovation in the development of values-based investing. Now, virtually any mutual fund family, 401(k) allocation, or variable annuity can be tailored to meet not only the financial objectives of the investor, but also match his or her personal values. This can be done regardless of whether there are any values-based mutual fund options in the fund family, 401(k), or variable annuity.

By first screening each of the mutual fund options to see what values are involved (i.e., tobacco, pornography, abortion, etc.), and then combining that information with the Nobel Prize-winning science of Modern Portfolio Theory (MPT), investors can attempt to achieve both a financial objective and a moral objective with the money they invest. No longer is there any legitimate reason for any investor to have to watch his or her money go one way while their personal values go the other.

WHAT ARE MY
VALUES-BASED INVESTMENTS OPTIONS?

Now that you know something about how your personal values can be translated into your investing, let's look at the types of available financial products from which you may choose. As you now know from the previous chapters, the phenomenon of values-based investing is still relatively new, but growing rapidly. In fact, I'll go on record here as suggesting that by the year 2004, regardless of where you do your investing or whom you use as a financial advisor, the question, *"Do you want your personal values reflected in your investment decisions?"* will be part of virtually every financial product purchase process.

By the time you read this book, chances are likely that the options available to you will be more comprehensive than what is presented here. I suggest referring to moneyandvalues.com, as well as the other Internet sites listed in this book for more up-to-the-minute information on available values-based products.

This chapter will describe some of the categories of values-based investment opportunities without delving into the dynamics of the product itself (for a more complete understanding of various investment and insurance products, please refer to Section III of this book).

The process of: (1) selecting your personal values; (2) evaluating your existing investments in light of your values; and (3) locating correlative investment and insurance products, would be an impossible task were it not for technology. However, with the new Internet site moneyandvalues.com, this comparative process becomes simple and efficient. Scheduled to be live in late 2000, moneyandvalues.com promises to make values-based investing an easy process for all investors and advisors.

Additionally, the patented technology developed by Exterprise (featured on the Discovery Channel program "Technology Today"), allows moneyandvalues.com to become a customized option for banks, credit unions, broker dealers and even online trading services. Suffice it to say that technology is making the idea of values-based investing a very practical and available tool for any investor or advisor.

MUTUAL FUNDS

By far the greatest number of investment options available by product category for values-based investing is mutual funds. The fund industry has recently proliferated with new asset classes, new investment managers and new values-screening criteria and there is no end in sight. The primary reason is, of course, the overall popularity and efficiency of mutual funds as an available investment vehicle. The popularity of mutual funds is also being buttressed by the popularity of the 401(k)

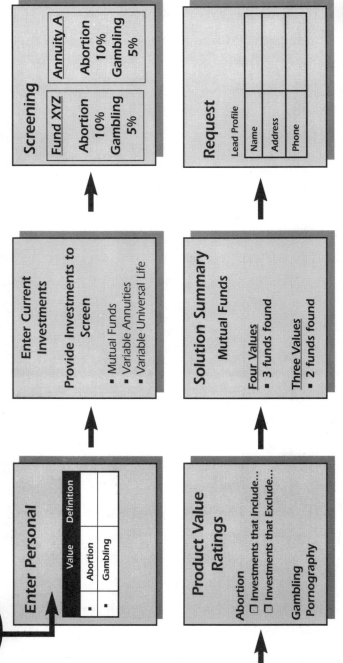

Moneyandvalues.com Flow Chart

Start

Enter Personal

Value	Definition
▪ Abortion	
▪ Gambling	

Enter Current Investments

Provide Investments to Screen

- Mutual Funds
- Variable Annuities
- Variable Universal Life

Screening

Fund XYZ	Annuity A
Abortion 10%	Abortion 10%
Gambling 5%	Gambling 5%

Product Value Ratings

Abortion
☐ Investments that Include...
☐ Investments that Exclude...

Gambling
Pornography

Solution Summary

Mutual Funds

Four Values
- 3 funds found

Three Values
- 2 funds found

Request

Lead Profile

Name	
Address	
Phone	

Cont.

INVESTMENT SCREENING

ACME Adv Mid Cap Instl
FMCCX

Overall Rating
16.21%

Morningstar Investment Objective
Mid-Cap Growth

Non-Marriage Lifestyle	5.12%
Alcohol	2.1%
Pornography	12.2%
Tobacco	4.9%
Abortion	5.7%
Gaming	7.00%
Nuclear Power	9.2%
Environment	11.8%
Defense Contractor	6.1%
Affirmative Action	6.6%

SAMPLE RATING
Ratings shown are for demonstration purposes only.

retirement plan, which utilizes mutual funds as its primary investment option. So, how do you begin to determine which values-based mutual fund is right for you? There are two parts to the answer to this question. One is financial and the other is values-based.

A mutual fund will offer its investors the opportunity to gain from the efficiency of pooled investments, immediate redemptions, diversification, and professional management. Additionally, each mutual fund will represent a particular style (growth, balanced, value, hybrid, etc.), and/or asset class (bonds, domestic equities, Latin America small capitalization, etc.).

The task of determining which (1) manager, (2) style, and (3) asset class are best for you can be daunting. Therefore, I recommend that you start from the standpoint of your overall investment and financial planning objective ("What rate of return do I need?", "What is my risk temperament?"), and work with a professional financial advisor who can guide you through the maze of options available to you.

Next, you will need to take your personal values into consideration. With what issues are you most concerned—abortion, pornography, the environment, nuclear power, affirmative action, etc.? Once you have a good handle on what your financial objectives are (previous paragraph), you then can search for that criteria in a values-screened version that reflects your personal values.

Given the tremendous variations and possible combinations, if it were not for technology, this process would probably overwhelm even the most zealous investor. But with Internet sites such as moneyandvalues.com integrating all of the components of the process, designing and managing a mutual fund portfolio that attempts to help you reach your financial objectives, and reflect your personal values becomes fairly simple.

Mutual Fund Wrap

Although there are values-based mutual funds representing nearly all of the asset classes and styles and managed by a wide range of professional managers, one of the most efficient methods of investing in mutual funds is through wrap programs.

A mutual fund wrap account or program combines a number of mutual funds representing several different asset classes, styles and even managers in an effort to provide the investor benefits of asset allocation. This could result in a "smoother ride" along your investment journey since you have the advantage of Modern Portfolio Theory working for you. (For more details on this portfolio management technique, please refer to Section III, "Integrating Values into Your Financial Plan").

Additionally, wrap programs offer a wide range of values screening criteria, which gives you the ability to further customize your investment program.

401(K) RETIREMENT PLANS

Closely related to mutual funds are the retirement plans that offer them as primary investment options. The 401(k) plan (and its nonprofit counterpart the 403(b)) have dramatically increased the net worth of millions of American workers over the last decade. However, only recently did 401(k) plans begin to offer participants values-based mutual fund options. The popularity of doing so has been documented in a survey by Yankelovich Partners, which was reported in the October 1999 edition of *Pension & Investment News*.

Paraphrasing the results, the survey asked employee participants if they were offered a socially responsible (values-based) mutual fund option in their 401(k) plan would they invest in it. The answer was that 70% of the participants indicated that they would. Then, Yankelovich researched the 401(k) plans that existed and included such a socially responsible option to see what percentage of the plan participants did, in fact, invest in the socially responsible option and they found that (guess what?) 70% of the participants were invested in that fund.

The growth of socially responsible mutual funds in 401(k) plans has not been without controversy, however. We heard a story from a financial advisor who had a client who was a senior executive with Ford Motor Company. Apparently, consistent with the growing popularity of socially responsible investing, Ford decided to offer a socially responsible fund in its 401(k) plan. However, this advisor's client was a social conservative, and the SRI option that Ford added to the plan was decidedly socially liberal. The client was livid that although social liberals would now be able to support their value system in the way that they invested in their 401(k) plan, social conservatives (like him) were not able to reflect their values. This apparent dilemma is not unique and, in fact, comes with the territory.

The answer to the dilemma lies in either offering both socially conservative and socially liberal mutual fund options, for example funds from Calvert, or Domini (socially liberal) and funds from Shepherd Values (socially conservative). The other option involves an innovative allocation program that is also being utilized with variable annuities.

A 401(k) plan can utilize the values screening of a service such as moneyandvalues.com to create a Personal Values Profile for the employee participant. That values profile is combined with the financial objectives of the client (risk, return, etc.) and the artificial intelligence then develops an asset allocation using the 401(k) mutual funds that attempts to reach both the financial objectives of the participant while also reflecting personal values. Using this approach, sometimes it may not be possible to attain a 100% compliance with the participants' values, because most (if not all) of the funds in the allocation are not values-based funds. Instead, participants may have to settle for 90% or 95% compliance with their values.

At the time of this writing, plans are underway to make this technology available to all 401(k) plans with an Internet-based platform starting with the innovative plans offered by DailyAccess.com. Most changes to the investment options available through 401(k) plans come as a result of employee participants requesting a specific option. If you would like your 401(k) plan to offer a values-based mutual fund option, contact your benefits administration office. Be sure to be specific about which values-based fund you want added, and it wouldn't hurt to get a few signatures from fellow plan participants to go along with yours.

The other option is to suggest to your plan sponsor that they add the values-based allocation technology described above. For more information on that option contact moneyandvalues.com.

Although there has been a dramatic increase in the number of retirement plans offering values-based options in the market today, unfortunately that does not seem to be the case in the areas where one would think that values-based investing would be of the highest concern. For example, most independent churches, Christian organizations, and conservative business enterprises do not even attempt yet to align their retirement plan investing with their values. Sounds preposterous, doesn't it? Imagine an organization or ministry that is "out to teach the world" about "values," but then invests its employees' retirement money into companies involved in pornography, abortion, and in support of a same-sex lifestyle. Believe it or not this is commonplace.

I will say in their defense that until recently there have been few fund options from which these socially conservative organizations could choose. Additionally, the process of adding funds to a qualified retirement plan such as a 403(b) or 401(k) can take a considerable amount of time and involve numerous committees and decision-making points. So it may be that the values-based phenomenon just hasn't been available as a legitimate option in the past.

Nonetheless, I have been involved personally in meetings where there just didn't seem to be an interest in developing consistency between the message that the organization preaches and the values represented by the money its retirement plan invests. I hope that attitude changes, as I think it will.

On the positive side, many of these churches and organizations are getting this message out to their members and affiliates through programs that offer this book and its counterpart, *Money for Life*, as an affinity benefit. At least that way each individual can educate himself or herself and take whatever course of action deemed most appropriate to their individual situation.

Variable Insurance Products

Although a lot of the financial media tends to turn its collective nose up at variable products, the fact is that they are very popular methods of providing for retirement and insurance. They enjoy tax-favored treatment on the investment gain by the IRS (tax deferral and, in some cases with variable universal life, tax free), and a very efficient method of accessing multiple funds, managers, styles and asset classes.

In a way, variable annuities and variable universal life contracts work similar to 401(k) plans in that they offer the investor numerous investment options. In the case of the 401(k) plan, those options are mutual funds. In the case of variable products, the options are close cousins of mutual funds, but are called "subaccounts," or "separate accounts." Therefore, when considering reflecting your values in a variable annuity or life contract, you are faced with the same options mentioned in the previous section.

Many variable products have recently added values-based sub-accounts to their options in the last few years. In fact, virtually all of the most popular variable products offer at least one values-based sub-account in their contract. However, here again, I know of only one variable annuity that offers a socially conservative values-based option, whereas I know of literally dozens that offer a socially liberal version. The objective, of course, should be to reach a balance. Shepherd Financial Services is aggressively attempting to have its socially conservative funds added to insurance companies' variable product portfolios as a balance to their socially liberal counterpart, and it appears they will succeed.

Additionally, some variable products offer a values-based allocation program similar to what was described in the section on 401(k) plans. The Values-In-Action Investment Allocation program, for example, is actually not a part of any variable product, but is offered as a service by a registered investment advisor. At the time of this writing, it is offered exclusively as a compliment to the Western Reserve Life variable annuity and variable universal life contracts by financial advisors who are members of the Values Financial Network.

Look for innovations in the coming year that will elevate a number of variable products to the point where you will be able to confidently reflect your values in the way that you invest in these popular products.

FIXED ANNUITIES AND LIFE INSURANCE

Where there are no mutual funds or separate accounts to screen, creating a values-based product becomes more difficult and requires a degree of creativity. For example, the Shepherd Values Annuities underwritten by Equitable of Iowa (an ING company) are not screened at all. Instead, they allow the customer to choose an "affinity organization" from a list of approved values-conscious groups such as Promise Keepers, Compassion International, Women of Faith, etc. As Shepherd Financial Services makes contributions to these organizations it attempts to reflect the wishes of its customers in its philanthropy.

As I have pointed out many times in this book, the values-based industry is engaged in tremendous innovation at present. In the next year I expect numerous fixed annuity and life insurance products to be developed that offer both the affinity program—such as the Shepherd Values Annuities—as well as an underlying screened investment portfolio. Within the last few months, I have been contacted by companies that are currently embarked on that initiative, so I know first hand what is coming down the pike. It is truly revolutionary and exciting!

OTHER VALUES-BASED PRODUCTS

Capitalism and the free market don't allow too many vacuums for too long. Where there is demand you can expect the market to produce an economic solution. Capital One® found that out. As one of the largest producers of credit cards in the world, Capital One® aggressively markets their credit cards on an affinity basis. From their Christian Faith Capital One® card, to a

credit card that supports sports fishing, Capital One®
allows credit card users to support their values and interests while using their credit card services.

Given the demand in the market and the culture for
opportunities to invest one's money in a way that reflects
his or her values, you can expect to see the following
values-based products being developed soon:

- Individual stock and bond portfolios

- Values-based online trading

- Long-term care insurance

- Medicare supplement

- Property and casualty insurance

The exciting reality is that any time someone invests or
spends his or her money, there exists an opportunity to
reflect that person's values. The financial instruments that
can be morphed into values-based versions are endless.

If you are interested in obtaining an updated list of
new values-based products, you may find the information at http://www.moneyandvalues.com helpful.

Section III
Integrating Values into Your Financial Plan

A financial planner has access to state-of-the-art technology that indicates clearly what the issues are, so that solutions to the tough choices involved in accomplishing life goals can be found.

CHAPTER 8

Financial Planning Explained

In Section I of this book, we discussed what is meant by values-based investing. We learned how financial products can be screened for certain values or issues, and how the research is accomplished.

In Section II, we dove into the mechanics of just how an investment can become a reflection of someone's value system, and how it actually can be designed and managed with specific values in mind. The information in both Section I and Section II is vital to a comprehensive understanding of values-based investing.

Section III, on the other hand, is not so much about the particulars of personal values as it is about the practicality of financial planning. In the final analysis, having the knowledge to do something without the blueprint for how to do it renders that knowledge superfluous. In the remaining chapters of *Your Money, Your Values,* I will present a case for financial planning. Although I continue to believe strongly that virtually everyone should work with a financial advisor (and I attempt to make that case, too), whether you take advantage of those professional services or not, approaching your investing from the perspective of a comprehensive financial plan will ultimately provide for better coordination, greater efficiency, and a more satisfactory financial result.

REASONS TO USE A FINANCIAL PLANNER

Before I drill down the specifics of developing a comprehensive financial plan, I first want to encourage you to consider taking advantage of the services of a professional. Whether you choose someone who is "certified" or not, whether you want a commission-only advisor, a fee-only advisor, or a hybrid of the two, in my opinion, you only can gain by partnering with a professional financial planner.

Technology

One of the first reasons to work with a professional is that the advisor/planner has access to sophisticated and comprehensive financial planning software. Information from three different dimensions of a personal information questionnaire is integrated into a "personal profile" from which decisions can be made. Through complex mathematical computations, the report shows the planner the kinds of things the client will need to change about the present allocation of financial resources to accomplish his or her future financial goals.

For example, let's say you want to retire at age sixty-five with an income of $3,400 a month. But after calculating your various assets, their current funding levels, and projected rates of return, it appears that you are going to be short of reaching your goal. One of the reasons has to do with the impact of inflation, historically at around 3.5% a year. So, at age sixty-five, the $3,400 becomes $7,748 in inflated dollars. When you fall short of your goal you are presented with two options: Either you can (a) increase your rate of return on your current investments; or (b) increase the amount of your contribution to the investments. If we assume that you have no additional money you could use to supplement your monthly investing, that means you'll have to increase the rate of return on your investments.

After reviewing your Investment Risk Profile, your planner determines that you are a fairly conservative investor who can't handle more than a 5% to 10% swing in your return. You say, "Yes, that's right." You may even turn to your spouse and ask, "Honey, what do you think?"

She raises up in her chair with an indignant attitude, "No, I'm not comfortable with a 5% to 10% loss to my principal. Are you actually talking about losing money? I'm not going to lose money."

With this response, if I were the planner, I would know that I have my work cut out for me, because you can't get there with the financial resources, risk profile, and attitude they have. The math just doesn't work.

If I were your planner, I might respond, "Okay, but without taking some amount of risk, we're going to have to construct a very conservative portfolio with a return expectation of only somewhere in the 5% to 10% range."

You glance up and say, "Okay."

I continue, "Well, you want to retire at age sixty-five with $3,400 a month of inflation-adjusted income, you don't have any additional money to invest, and you will not agree to a slightly higher volatility level of investing. That means we have only one option left. You will have to wait to retire...about nine years."

"No, we can't," they say in unison. "We've been planning our retirement for a long time. We don't know when our health may fail, and we have to be able to retire at sixty-five!"

These clients have unrealistically negative perceptions about risk, given their investment time frame. They can handle a greater swing in their portfolio, probably as high as 15 percent. What they need more than anything is education—education about tough choices, risk management, and financial planning. Left without this education, many people will take the starvation approach to investing and money management.

A financial planner has access to state-of-the-art technology that indicates clearly what the issues are, so that solutions to the tough choices involved in accomplishing life goals can be found.

Expertise of Financial Planner

The second reason to utilize a financial planner is because of his or her expertise. A qualified planner should know a great deal of information that the clients do not know and cannot access. The planner should be able to devise creative solutions that benefit the clients in ways better than those they could create with their own resources.

Many clients, for example, make a pivotal mistake. They believe if their investments are divided among two to five different mutual funds that they are adequately diversified. However, statistics show that in order to reduce overall portfolio volatility, investors should opt for more than an arbitrary allocation of money over different mutual funds. They also need a proper asset allocation, that is, having their money invested in several asset classes, such as U.S. stocks, small company stocks, international bonds, corporate bonds, and natural resources.

These various asset classes should be somewhat negatively correlated with each other so that when one of the asset classes suffers a market decline in its value, then another asset class in the same investment portfolio might be gaining. Over time, the end result will be solid returns accompanied with lower overall volatility.

The academic body of knowledge supporting this technology of portfolio management has won two Nobel prizes in economic science and is employed by most of the world's pension plan managers. Without an expensive and highly sophisticated software program, continuously updated, coupled with a high degree of portfolio management competency, you will not be able to construct and manage this type of portfolio.

Specialized World

The third reason you should take advantage of a financial professional is because today's world has become specialized. No consumer (no matter how sophisticated or well read) can become familiar with the vast variety of financial instruments sold today. Additionally, no consumer can distinguish thoroughly the benefits and disadvantages of each investment opportunity, and then prudently determine how much to invest and over what period of time.

Admittedly, it's certainly possible for an individual to develop a do-it-yourself financial plan. That doesn't mean it's a wise thing to do. By definition that plan will be 'dumbed down' to the individual's level of expertise and resource accessibility.

Competent financial advice is similar to other professional advice and services, such as medical, legal, or accounting. The fact is, most often the results obtained on your own will not approach the benefits of having utilized the services of a competent professional.

Professional Discipline

The fourth reason, if you are like most human beings, you lack the discipline to stay the course of your financial plan without a professional's help. When we have a financial crisis, our conviction to develop a financial plan grows. Then, after the crisis subsides, we revert to our normal life—the kids have soccer practice, the muffler on the car needs replacement, the house needs repainting, the grandparents visit for summer vacation, etc. In the meantime, our financial plan begins to lose its sense of urgency.

One of my financial planner friends in Canada says, "If you have a problem, turn it into a procedure and you won't have that problem any more." If you lack a systematic plan to meet your financial needs and wants, the procedure is to locate a professional financial planner to manage the process.

BEYOND THE MYTHS: DEVELOPING A FINANCIAL PLAN

Mirrors are a good metaphor for the first step of the financial planning process. Some people naturally gravitate toward them, touching their hair and checking their physique every time they walk past one. Other people know they won't like what they would see, so they rush past any mirror that confronts them. Once you know how you want to manifest the values that motivate your life, then you are ready to plan that life with questions such as:

- Do I want a family? If so, when?

- Will either my spouse or I stay home with the young children?

- What kind of career do I want and how long do I want to work at it?

- Do I want to take a year or two out of my career for personal time?

- What kind of a philanthropy program do I want to establish?

At this point, you're ready to take the next step—an honest look in the mirror and an assessment of your current life plan. Without that look in the mirror, you are not operating with full information and will only be able to reach your life goals serendipitously!

A couple from Hermitage, Tennessee, came to see me. As we talked, I learned they were in their late fifties and facing retirement in about four years. Over the years, they had never had a relationship with a financial planner. As they considered retirement, they understood that the move from the accumulation phase of life to the distribution phase would require some professional help. At this point in time, they needed to consider their investments within the context of life expectancy, integrating considerations of risk, return, and taxes. So the couple filled out the Personal Information Form, and we began the process of analyzing their current financial picture.

In a subsequent meeting, I presented them with some tough choices. Based on their Investment Risk Profile, I knew they didn't like anything invested in the stock market. I explained, "Based on what you are telling me, you will have to think about reducing your expectations for retirement income. You will not be able to live as you dreamed about, or in a manner you had been anticipating."

For about an hour, we talked about these issues and how their choices will impact their retirement dreams. They didn't like any of the possibilities. Armed with the information, they took it home to think about. One of my suggestions was to move half of their retirement assets into market-based investments (which would fluctuate in value). They didn't like that suggestion, but they also had a great dislike for the looming possibility of having to change their lifestyle. Their current investments were in certificates of deposit (CDs), savings accounts, and fixed annuities.

At their next appointment, the couple wanted to learn more about this market-based investment approach. I explained the concept of investing in the market using a strategy referred to as asset allocation. Simplified, such a strategy would allocate portions of their money into several different classes or categories of investments on a diversified basis. We would invest in different sized companies, different industries, some stocks, some bonds, and even different countries, as I made reference to in the earlier example. The body of academic research supporting this strategy is called Modern Portfolio Theory (MPT). Using this science, it's the least risky method of entering the market. After a long discussion, they were willing to take the plunge so they could attempt to preserve their current lifestyle.

Unfortunately, I gave this advice in late 1993, when the markets had been good. Although I rarely talked about what happened in the markets over the recent months because of its historic irrelevancy in the long run, these clients were well aware of the above-average returns for the past year.

However, in 1994, the Federal Reserve did something unprecedented. Five times in that year, they raised interest rates—which is the death knell for the market. Over those twelve months, the market performed very poorly. Now I had put 50 percent of this couple's retirement assets into market-based investments. Throughout the year, the couple came into the office with long faces that reflected their anxiety and discouragement. I kept saying, "Hang in there. Trust the science. Trust the math and the history." During that first year, I did a lot of handholding.

The second year, they had good returns—in fact, excellent. The third and fourth years were excellent also. In fact, so good were the returns that their confidence in the markets grew roots. Then, during one of our annual reviews, these people—so risk-averse that they almost opted for a pittance in retirement income over having to accept market risk—actually asked me, "Can we move all of our money into the market?"

Today almost all of their retirement funds have been reallocated from fixed instruments to market-based investments. Their portfolio has grown so much that what began small is now large. Even if they lose 15% of the large sum, they still have much more profit than they ever would have had in the fixed market. But it was tough going the first year as this couple considered a new approach to investing. The learning process for them, as with most people, wasn't instantaneous.

The first prudent decision this couple made was to look into the mirror. The reflection they saw initially made them quite uncomfortable. The next positive step they took was to seek professional assistance. After making appropriate changes, they no longer feared looking into the mirror. We'll discuss more about mirrors—the financial planning process—later. But first, let's qualify the professional help that may be needed.

CHOOSING THE RIGHT FINANCIAL PLANNER

A financial planner is the qualified professional who can help you appropriate your financial resources in a way that will support your life goals. This person may be young, old, male, or female. You need to spend a serious amount of time interviewing financial planners. You may only need to interview from two to four planners to choose the appropriate one for you. Interview a variety of planners so that you have a taste of the various personality types, styles of practice, and fee schedules.

There is plenty of room for varying personalities and styles, but there are also certain fundamentals that should be nonnegotiable. Let's review some of them.

Full-Time Professional

A qualified financial planner must be engaged in the business full-time, not part-time. Preferably, the planner is associated with a firm of other professionals. Then, if necessary, he or she can call on others for additional assistance in their areas of specialty.

You may find it helpful to have a prepared list of questions when interviewing financial planners. These questions could include:

- How long have you been practicing this profession?

- What type of success have you achieved?

- How many clients do you have? (I would be hesitant to work with someone who had fewer than fifty clients. However, if the median client profile is $2 million of net worth, then it might be reasonable for that particular financial planner to only have twenty-five clients.)

- What does the median client profile look like? (You would want that profile to describe you.)

- What licenses do you hold? (The National Association of Security Dealers (NASD) licenses individuals to transact business in the U.S. Registration is not optional; the law requires it. The process involves written examinations and continuing education. Also, the planner should have a life insurance and a health insurance license.)

- What professional designations do you have? (Financial planning requires competency in a wide range of subdisciplines, including investments, insurance, estate planning, and income taxation.)

The College of Financial Planning in Denver, Colorado, is the only independent academic institution with the purpose of certifying financial planners. Under the operation of the National Endowment for Financial Education (NEFE), the college has established a rigorous curriculum to test for competency in each area of financial planning: insurance and risk management, investment planning, income taxes, retirement planning, and estate planning.

After each course of study, the candidate takes a test. When a candidate has successfully passed each area of study, then he or she completes a two-day, ten-hour comprehensive examination. This test is demanding.

The last time I checked, the pass rate for the examination was only 52 percent.

Certification for a candidate is achieved only after successful completion of the examinations, a personal background check from the college, and achievement of a level of vocational experience. Only after a candidate has fulfilled these requirements, is the status of Certified Financial Planner (CFP) granted.

Because of the rigorous educational curriculum, as well as the academic integrity of the entire program, I recommend considering the CFP credential for your advisor. I am not a big fan of what the College for Financial Planning does beyond administering a rigorous curriculum, but I am an advocate of their academic integrity. And although the CFP credential should be a consideration, there may be very legitimate reasons for choosing someone who does not have that particular credential.

While there are other license designations, such as ChFC (Chartered Financial Consultant) or CLU (Chartered Life Underwriter) or LUTC (Life Underwriters Training Council), in my opinion, these licenses are not as comprehensive or intellectually demanding as a CFP. There are probably a dozen other designations that you'll see on financial planners' business cards, but most of these are more along the order of belonging to a trade association than reflective of academic achievement. Also, these other designations may be biased toward the life insurance industry.

Keep in mind that attorneys and accountants are not financial planners. Unfortunately, most of them will jump at the chance to give you their opinions on the subject, but they have neither academic training nor experience in the field to back their opinions.

Business Environment

Who is actually going to process the business? Does the planner have a staff? Is the planner a one-person operation? Does he or she meet you in your home, or at the office? If a planner is doing a good job for his or her clients, then staff support will be needed. The financial planning business is extremely management intensive. You don't want your planner spending his or her time doing paperwork, filing, and keeping up with administrative details. Instead, you want the planner to spend that valuable time thinking creatively and learning about new and better planning strategies.

It's acceptable for a planner to work from home, but a separate office is preferable. Outside office space is another concrete measure of planner's the client base and commitment to serving clients in a professional manner. Separate office space communicates that your planner is willing to spend several thousand dollars each month to develop a professional presence and transact business in a professional way.

In most cases, the highly regulated securities industry strictly prohibits representatives from recommending any product not offered through the broker-dealer that he or she represents. This can limit the scope of a planner's capacity to meet your needs, particularly if the broker-dealer is associated with an insurance company, or is small. I advise finding a professional who is associated with an independent broker-dealer that offers insurance and investments from hundreds of different product sponsors. This way the professional can offer multiple options in all the mainstream financial product categories. Then you can gain the benefit of the firm's research into the various competing products in the marketplace.

Chemistry

This qualification for a planner is less tangible, but it is an absolutely necessary part of the selection process. Otherwise, the relationship is doomed to failure. The chemistry has to go both directions. Not only does the client have to feel comfortable the planner, but the planner also must want to work with the client. On occasion, I have turned away potential clients simply because the chemistry didn't work.

About four years ago, an older woman telephoned me and said, "My husband and I are interviewing financial planners. My husband is about seventy years old, and we need some assistance. We'd like to make an appointment to see you."

When I met the couple, the husband looked very stern and cold. I tried to be warm and develop some chemistry and common ground for discussion. But this man wanted nothing to do with it. He positioned me at the head of the table, then pointed to my right for his wife to sit, and then he sat at my left. He got out three typed, single-spaced sheets of paper that listed his assets and placed a copy in front of each of us. For the next twenty minutes, he read the list and justified why each asset in his portfolio had been purchased. Then he looked at me and said, "Today I'm here to find out from you what you would change and why."

Immediately I could tell the relationship was not going to work. This man didn't want my counsel; he was looking for an argument. And even if I "won" on this day, the arguments would continue for years to come. My guess is that this argumentative, combative style was formed as a part of his personality many years ago. With my kindest effort, I worked my way out of the situation. I terminated the meeting saying, "I wish you well in your search for a financial planner."

The man, who had a net worth of over $1 million, looked shocked. Nonetheless, I had no interest in taking on that kind of client, regardless of how much money he had.

The lack of chemistry isn't always on the client side of things. I've met planners who are overbearing, arrogant, and demanding. Sometimes it goes to the other extreme;

some planners are so timid that you never receive any substance from them.

Education

It's important to understand that bankers, attorneys and Certified Public Accountants (CPAs) are not financial planners. While their professions can be important to the financial planning process, they are not specifically equipped to assist you with your financial goals. Most bankers have almost no formal education in financial planning. Attorneys are required to take only a few hours of education in estate planning to become a member of their respective bar associations. CPAs are accountants, not financial planners. CPAs do audits and tax returns, and even assist with business plans, but these skills do not provide them the academic base needed to help you develop a sound financial plan.

In the same line of reasoning, make sure you do not confuse intelligence with competency. A brain surgeon is highly educated in a very specific field and is likely very intelligent. However, because this doctor lacks the formal academic training in financial planning, he or she will be a less than competent financial advisor (whether the person admits it or not!).

Also, make sure you don't confuse trust and love with overall competency. Your father may love you deeply and, if you request his assistance in financial planning, may give you whatever information he has available to him, even if he has no specific training in the field. Unfortunately, his lack of competency will eventually cause you to have a financial plan with less-than-optimum performance. However, if you asked for his assistance in another area—say, heart surgery—he would immediately recognize his lack of competency and, motivated by love, refer you to a qualified heart surgeon (unless of course, he is a heart surgeon). You should exercise equal common sense in the area of financial planning.

As pointed out earlier, the financial planner should be competent and familiar with a wide range of such financial-planning subdisciplines, such as investments, insurance, income taxes, and estate planning.

What happens when you don't deal with a financial planner who is well versed on these subdisciplines? Your financial plan can become self-defeating. A couple of years ago I witnessed an example of this. Many people mistakenly believe that if someone has a high profile and makes a lot of money that person has excellent advisors. This assumption isn't necessarily true, and in many cases, it's exactly the opposite.

One of my clients, a high-profile sports figure, had a net worth of about $7 million, and an annual income of about $1 million. This man had been receiving advice from a stockbroker who knew nothing about insurance, or income taxes, or estate planning. When this client came to me, I discovered that he was paying profoundly high income taxes because no one had introduced him to tax-saving strategies. For every $1 million of income, he gave up $450,000 in taxes. I suggested a few alterations in his investing strategy that resulted in his next $1 million of income being taxed at only 20%. That represented a savings of $250,000 in one year because of proper financial advice.

As we worked with this client, we found that he had paid about $2,500 for estate planning advice that included a living trust and a life insurance trust. The fact that no one bothered to follow up and move the client's assets into the trusts meant that they were virtually worthless. Unless corrected, it appeared that the family would pay an additional $1.6 million in federal estate taxes.

In the area of insurance, the stockbroker turned over all insurance-related considerations to an insurance salesman. The insurance salesman buttonholed this high-profile client and convinced him to put $250,000 cash into a single premium whole life policy. The result of this mistake was substantial. It meant the internal rate of return on the $250,000 policy was only in the area of 2.5% to 3%! And because the insurance was not handled outside of the client's estate, it meant that as much as 55% of the death proceeds would be consumed by federal estate taxes. This decision was in no way a coordinated part of a well-thought financial plan.

From my point of view, having been an independent financial planner, this client was taken advantage of. The key broker was referring the client to other people in the company for insurance and estate planning—yet, because of his lack of competency in these fields, he had no way of ensuring there was an overall coordinated strategy to all the decisions.

The insurance agent, accountants, attorneys, and the broker were all making money from the client. Unfortunately, the client spent a great deal of financial resources with little to show for it. This sports figure expected his advisor to provide competent planning; but in fact, his advisor was not competent at all.

THE THREE IMPORTANT PRINCIPLES

Regardless of whether or not you choose to work with a planner who is a CFP, you need to develop and manage a financial plan that is customized to your specific life goals. Following are three principles to use in the search for professional assistance: (1) academic integrity; (2) product neutrality; and (3) plan management. The right planner will reflect these principles in working with you.

Academic Integrity

A well-developed financial plan begins like a science project. It integrates various pieces into a systematic whole in order to produce an effective result. That sounds complicated, but it really isn't. To simplify the understanding, sometimes it's easier to start by eliminating what financial planning is not.

- Financial planning is not simply a budget.

- Financial planning is not merely the purchase of an insurance policy or annuity.

- Financial planning is not just an investment account with a broker.

- Financial planning is not just the combination of a 401(k) and term life insurance.

Financial planning is the systematic management of your financial resources (cash, investments, retirement accounts, debts, insurance policies) toward the achievement of your particular life goals. It is the management of those resources in the most prudent manner to maximize their financial benefit as they relate to your financial goals. This process is dynamic, flexible, and evolutionary. We will discuss this principle in greater detail as it is reflected in the Comprehensive Financial Analysis.

Product Neutrality

Product neutrality is the second principle related to selecting professional assistance. Let's say that you want to buy a new car. You drive into a local Ford® dealership and begin talking with a salesperson. What brand of car do you think the salesperson will recommend? A Toyota®? A Chrysler®? I don't think so. Yet many people solicit financial advice in the same way. They turn to a salesperson who is associated with a company that only sells proprietary products.

You may have little or no problem finding a financial planner who shares your values, is a CFP with 200 clients, has all the necessary licenses, and has been in the business for five years. Sounds like the perfect candidate so far. But because this hypothetical planner works as a captive agent for an insurance company, what types of products do you think that planner will recommend to you? Regardless of what may be most beneficial for your situation, such planners are constrained by their relationship with the company. These planners have no choice but to recommend only their company's products.

Here's the critical question to ask yourself: Are these the products that you need? The problem is, you aren't really going to know. Bingo! That's why it's better if you work with an independent planner who is licensed through an independent broker-dealer.

Your financial planner should have access to a variety of investment and insurance companies. In fact, this planner should have access to virtually every type of financial instrument that possibly could be needed for a client who fits your profile. For example, the planner should be able to access multiple families of mutual funds, several insurance companies, and options for other types of programs such as tax credit programs, energy programs, limited partnerships, and a host of money managers.

Plan Management

The final element of our three important principles is plan management. Plan management will allow you maximum flexibility to handle change. Whether you want it or not, life will deal you many changes. And as you face life changes, you also want your financial plan to reflect these changes. As a minimum, you should meet with your financial planner annually to monitor your plan. Before this meeting, your planner should update all of your financial records and rerun all the analyses. Then during your meeting, you will have the necessary information to determine if your plan needs to be changed.

Too often, both consumers and financial services professionals make the mistake of investing many hours of research and discussion in order to produce a financial plan, only to walk away from it and never refer to it again.

WHEN THESE THREE ELEMENTS ARE NOT IN FOCUS

Academic integrity means you'll have a complete picture of your present situation, along with the available strategies you can use to make improvements. Product neutrality means that you'll have access to financial products such as mutual funds and insurance plans from many different companies. Plan management means that you'll have continual professional oversight of your plan to make sure that any changes that are required as you move forward are appropriately integrated into your plan in the years to come. This is how the financial planning process should work in a perfect world. But our world is not perfect.

Many years ago, I was a general agent for a large insurance and investment company and had only recently become a CFP. I found myself wrestling with the issue of developing financial plans based on academic integrity.

One day I got a phone call from a registered representative (a licensed individual who sells securities) who reported to me, "I've placed a good piece of business (meaning he had made some money), but the guy is sort of going backward on his decision. Can you come down and help me?"

"Sure," I said. Then I found out the name of the client. He was a senior pastor in the city—a scholarly gentleman who had helped thousands of people in their spiritual journey. Pastors are not paid well, and now this pastor was facing retirement in three or four years with inadequate financial resources.

Jerry had recommended a particular insurance-related investment program that was limited to four investment options. I agreed to meet with the pastor and Jerry, and I listened as Jerry extolled the virtues of this particular investment program. As they talked, the pastor's confidence in the program increased. But as I listened to Jerry's pitch, my discomfort increased.

As we sat around the pastor's dining room table, he finally took a deep breath and sighed. Then he sat back and said, "Okay, I'll keep the program. But I have one more question. There are four investment options in this program. Who is going to help me figure out which ones to put my money in and decide when I need to change that allocation? You know, for how long and what percentage of my money should go into each one?"

Jerry leaned across the table and said with self-inflated pomp, "That's where I come in." Now I knew for a fact that Jerry had about as much competency in that area as anybody off the street. Six months earlier this registered representative was selling jewelry behind the counter at a major retail chain! Certainly Jerry was a Christian, but that did not give him any special competency as an investment advisor.

I watched as this pastor entrusted his life savings to Jerry's management. Even under the best of circumstances with the best professional help in the world, the pastor was going to eke out only a meager retirement. The least he deserved was competent, professional assistance. But he didn't get that quality professional help. He got a former jewelry salesman who had been in the industry for six months.

I almost threw up at the scene, yet I was helpless to do anything about it. Nothing illegal had taken place, and the salesman had done precisely what his company had trained him to do—sell their products. I walked away from that meeting more determined than ever to educate people and do something about the future of financial planning. *Your Money, Your Values* is but one step in that direction.

SHARED VALUES SYSTEM

Does your planner have a values system that is consistent with yours? Values shouldn't be the only consideration, but your planner's values system should be a significant factor. In fact, I would rank it at least as high as licenses, years in the business, number of clients, and product neutrality.

Many people, however, make the mistake of putting so much emphasis on shared values that they fail to properly evaluate the other key qualifications. This mistake can and does lead to a lot of frustration, havoc, and unfulfilled goals down the road. At the Values Financial Network, we have a saying, "Do business with us because of the quality of work that we do. The fact that we share the same values can only enhance the relationship. It should not cause the relationship."

To illustrate this principle, consider a well-known Christian marketer who refers to himself as a financial advisor. This "expert" hosts a national radio program and has a following in the hundreds of thousands. Yet the only criterion that this person meets on my list of qualifications for financial planners is that he is a Christian. As a result, I have heard this marketer make numerous and substantial mistakes in his advice to people on his radio program. Because he doesn't adequately understand economics in general and financial planning in particular, he tends to present an apocalyptic vision of the economic future. In fact, his focus has most often been on telling people about the coming economic collapse and how they should prepare.

Consequently, the financial decisions that people are led to by this type of advice are often stunted, shortsighted, and uncoordinated. Imagine how dramatically different your financial decisions would be if they were based on a coming apocalypse. Because this marketer isn't licensed and has no industry professional certifications such as CFP, no regulatory body holds him accountable for his off-the-wall prognostications. So, although he meets the qualification of "shared values," he does not meet any of the other critical components of a professional financial planner.

How Are Financial Planners Compensated?

If you have diligently followed the advice in the previous section, it will be hard for you to make a mistake in this area. Among financial planners, there is a huge debate over this particular issue—and it will never be resolved.

Some planners prefer to charge a fee for their services and they feel strongly that to do so is the most objective approach. Other planners don't charge fees for planning. They are compensated through commissions on the sale of financial instruments. These planners feel their approach is more fair since clients are under no obligation to pay for service unless they implement a financial plan.

Fee-Only Financial Planners

Fee-only planners charge for their time, asserting in that ultimate neutrality in the product area is their advantage. In other words, they won't be motivated to recommend a high commission strategy to you since no commissions are involved. They contend that clients should opt to pay for the professional's time and expertise, which therefore would be unbiased. As a result, the clients, if they so choose, are free to go elsewhere to implement the plan.

But this strength of neutrality is also its weakness. For a financial plan to be effective, it has to be managed for many years to come. You want to be sure that your planner has an incentive not only to keep up with the academics involved in the planning process, but also with the changing financial product side. It is difficult to rationalize that a fee-only planner would be as motivated to continuously research tax credit programs, mutual funds, investment managers, insurance products, and all the rest of the product landscape if no compensation for implementing recommendations is involved.

According to the latest survey from the College for Financial Planning, the median cost of a financial plan is $800, but can amount to as much as $5,000. The median hourly rate is $95.*

Commission-Only Planners

Once the planner does the analysis, recommendations are made and then the plan is implemented. For example, you may have to purchase life insurance or invest in mutual funds, or you may need a tax credit program.

A commission is built into almost every single financial instrument. In nine times out of ten, even when you pay for "objective" advice, you will also pay a commission to implement your financial plan—whether it's to the firm that gives the advice or to another.

But let's consider the flip side of the fee-only approach. The other possibility is to use a commission-only planner whose advantage is that services are provided for free— in a sense. Actually, the planner can't get paid until you buy something, which naturally increases the incentive to sell you a particular product.

By definition, this planner cannot give you objective advice because if you don't really need to purchase anything, say for example life insurance, then in one sense you've taken away the planner's ability to be compensated. For this obvious reason, the commission-only type of planner is not necessarily the better choice.

* According to CFP Annual Survey, 1997 data.

My Own Hybrid Approach to the Compensation Issue

About four years ago, I created a hybrid approach that serves to balance the competing interests in the financial planning process. Most of the Values Financial Network affiliates will use an approach similar to the following.

For my staff and me to spend an appropriate amount of considered time with clients, we have to know that no matter what decisions are made, we will be fairly compensated. We charge our clients an average fee of $400, and for this fee the client receives a Comprehensive Financial Analysis and a Financial Organizer in a three-ring binder, and a minimum of four hours of our time. This approach allows me to pursue the process without the concern for having to make a sale. It also allows clients to receive a comprehensive analysis that they can choose to implement through us or to take elsewhere, and at a price that is 50% of the going rate.

Is the Proximity of the Financial Planner Important?

The exact location of your financial planner relative to your residence is unimportant. I have had clients scattered all across the nation. One of my clients is in the Dallas/Fort Worth, Texas, area. We have met only twice. I've not had a meeting with this client in over two years other than over the telephone. It was critical to establish rapport in a face-to-face session early in the process. But from that time on, we were able to proceed without requiring either party to travel.

My suggestion is that you locate a financial planner who works with an independent broker-dealer. The fees should be low enough to allow you to engage his or her services without it causing a major financial burden to the client.

The planner should have similar values to yours (more about this important topic later in the book), be someone you enjoy working with, and have associates who can be consulted for additional assistance.

How to Locate a Financial Planner

Call the Values Financial Network at 1-888-346-8258 to locate a financial planner, or log onto the VFN Internet site at http://www.moneyandvalues.com.

We have developed an extensive network of values-conscious financial planners who meet the above standards of professionalism and have been certified by the VFN to develop values-based financial plans.

*The process
needed to develop a
financial analysis sounds
complicated, but in reality
it's straightforward.*

CHAPTER 9

The Three-Step Process of Financial Planning

Now that you've selected your financial planner, what happens next? At the Values Financial Network, we recommend that financial planning be implemented as a three-step process.

INTRODUCTION TO FINANCIAL PLANNING: THE FIRST INTERVIEW

The first session, or initial interview, is complimentary. I've never heard of a planner who charges for this introductory session. This session will provide you with an opportunity to know more about the planner. He is going to explain his planning process. How will it be accomplished? Will there be other staff members with whom you will interface in this process? How much time will it require? What will it cost, and how will the fees be structured?

This is a get-acquainted session that lasts between thirty and sixty minutes. During that interview, the planner should ask why you are interested in financial planning and what specific things motivated you to do a financial plan. There may be a life event or personal issue that drives your motivation.

For example, a client may say, "I just moved into town," "I just changed jobs and got a big promotion," "I am thinking about buying a new house," or "I've received a large inheritance." Or it could be simply, "I'm not pleased with my current investment program." Any type of change in your personal life or your financial life may trigger a session with a planner. The planner will want to know about this motivation, and you should get some degree of comfort with his or her initial responses. You should not expect the planner to make specific recommendations—yet—but rather cover those issues in a broad conceptual manner.

At the end of the session, the planner will give you a homework assignment. You will need to complete a Personal Information Form (see Appendix A).

The financial analysis creates a complete picture. Remember the mirror? Your financial plan starts there. Don't be bashful, step right up and stare. Stare with the confidence that regardless of your degree of comfort with what you may see initially, once you've completed the process, for the rest of your life you will be at peace with the reflection when you look in the mirror.

The process needed to develop a financial analysis sounds complicated, but in reality it's straightforward.

Two overriding dimensions need to be fully considered. One involves taking inventory of your financial resources; the other involves identifying your goals and objectives. As in the case of a vacation, if you fail to appropriately consider both dimensions, either you'll end up halfway through without any money, or you'll have money, but not be enjoying it as you could.

The questions you'll need to address when completing the Personal Information Form require an honest look at your current financial situation. It is important to pay attention to accuracy, even if requires a bit of effort on your part to gather the necessary information.

Often we have this sort of information in a variety of places. The value of such information comes when you pull it into an integrated document for study. To help you become familiar with this process, I've included an example of this questionnaire in Appendix A.

Some of this information isn't located easily and will cause some frustration in finding it, so be prepared. Some of the information will be in your bank checkbook, but it will need to be reconstructed. Some of it may need to come from your accountant or attorney. Some may come from the benefits administration department at your job. Some of it may even be gathering dust on the top of your refrigerator. (Yes, one of my clients actually stuck his life insurance policy on top of the refrigerator and forgot about it!) If the information isn't readily available, then figure out how to get it.

Incidentally, don't make the process any more tedious than it has to be. For example, there are no grades given on the form for penmanship. In fact, sometimes you don't have to fill in every blank if you provide supplemental materials like copies of insurance policies, account statements, and retirement-account reports. The point is to provide thorough information.

I always warn people in advance about this process. First, it isn't fun. You are not going to enjoy it, so be prepared for that from the beginning. You will have to appropriate time from your life for the purpose, probably from two to four hours. The good news, though, is that once you complete this form, you will never have to complete it again. From that point forward, it is simply a matter of updating the records.

The first portion of the process involves objective information about your current financial situation. For example, you will need to list your various assets (separately for husband, wife, and jointly held property), including:

- Retirement accounts

- Investments

- Insurance contracts

- Checking account

- Savings account

- Money Market accounts

- Personal property, including your residence and automobile(s)

The second portion is more subjective and deals with what you want the money to do for your life. This section includes such questions as:

- When do you want to retire? What will you do during retirement?

- How much money do you want to have when you retire?

- Do you want to help your children through college? How much money do you want to give them?

- Are you planning for a second home?

- Are you planning for a change in residence?

- Do you want to set aside appropriate funds for recreation such as a boat or horses or an avocation?

- Do you have any significant gifts that you want to make? To the church? To a mission?

- Is there a period of time in your life when you would not like to work in order to serve in the mission field, study some subject, go to school, or help an ailing family member?

- Do you have plans to begin your own business? For you or your spouse, or both?

- Are you going to have children? Do you want one spouse to stay home and, if so, for how long?

These questions are not exhaustive, but they acquaint you with some of the possibilities for consideration in this process.

As I consider how some people think about financial goals, I have a favorite saying—"Some people tiptoe through life so they can arrive at death safely." Many times people take this approach toward their financial planning. These people believe that life must be lived "accurately," as if there is some kind of supernatural blueprint that must be followed. Following this line of reasoning may, in fact, keep you from becoming overextended, or unemployed, but it may also cause you to miss out on what real life was meant to be.

Each one of us has the freedom to pursue our own way through life. Individual goals vary in length, structure, specificity, and resources. There is no correct standard for when to retire, for how much to help with your child's college education, or for whether you should enter a second career. What a joy it is to live every day in the knowledge that God breathed life into us as individuals, knowing us even before we were born, and that nothing can separate us from the love of God. What a passion for life we have when we desire to live a life of purpose, reflecting God's creativity, love, and joy throughout our life plan as it evolves.

Don't be too demanding of yourself for hard and fast goals. Keep in mind that life is dynamic and that no matter what goals you establish, you will change and refine them over a period of time. The central purpose of goal setting is to establish a clear direction. Take a few moments to consider what you want to have in your future and when you want it to happen.

Your goals don't have to be singular. You can have four or five simultaneous goals—retirement, a second home, sending somebody through college, maybe taking four years off. Each of these goals can require a different time horizon and a different investment strategy. The key lies in flexibility and individualization. You should follow the plan and strategy that are right for you.

One of the most critically important objectives for a financial planner is to free people from feeling the need to fit their life into someone else's preconceived idea. As the saying goes, life is not a dress rehearsal. This is it. The life you are living now and planning for in the future is the only one you get. So do it your way, as a natural outgrowth and reflection of your relationship with God.

MINI-MARATHON: THE SECOND INTERVIEW

The second session with your planner generally lasts from two to two-and-a-half hours. During this session, the planner will review the details of your financial situation with you line by line and page by page.

All of the effort you put into filling out the Personal Information Form will bear fruit in the form of a Comprehensive Financial Analysis. The Comprehensive Financial Analysis will be the basis for determining whether you are on track to reach your goals or whether you'll need to make some changes.

Your financial analysis should be comprehensive and unbiased. You need to be able to see the entire picture before you can make any decisions. Keep in mind that any analysis that a salesperson uses specifically to market a particular financial product (such as life insurance, annuities, or stocks) may have a bias toward the particular product built into the result.

A true Comprehensive Financial Analysis should include the following:

- Personal values analysis
- Cash flow report
- Net worth statement
- Insurance analysis
- Income tax projection
- Investment portfolio analysis
- Retirement income projection
- Education funding report
- Estate transfer report

As these reports are reviewed, the planner will be giving you suggestions, strategies, options, and solutions for you to consider. The session requires a great deal of interaction between you and the planner. Typically, at the end of this session you feel like the Gary Larson cartoon character who, sitting in a classroom, raises his hand and says, "Teacher, may I be excused? My brain is full." Hopefully, your planner will summarize the discussion and recommend a course of action.

One caution for this step in the process: Don't get caught up in "analysis paralysis." Fear of making a mistake can totally immobilize some people, rendering them unable to do anything. If this happens to you, remember an adage from the book *In Search of Excellence*: "Disorganized action is always preferable to organized inaction." The key is to do something.

At the end of this mini-marathon, you and your financial planner will have decided on a route for designing and implementing a financial plan.

PLAN IMPLEMENTATION: THE THIRD INTERVIEW

Either during the mini-marathon or in a telephone conversation, decisions have been made about such things as life insurance, investment portfolio, retirement strategies, tax-reduction techniques, and so forth. Each one of these decisions triggers some paperwork to implement the new strategy. This paperwork probably will be handled by one of the financial planner's staff at the office, through the mail, or by the fax machine.

At the third meeting, all the numbers from the initial financial analysis will have been reworked to include the recommended changes. For example, during this third session you will not find a gap between your retirement goals and the strategy to reach those goals (unlike your opening session when you didn't yet have a plan). You and your planner will have created the means to reach those goals.

At this time any contracts, policies, or new account statements will be added to your financial organizer, which will become your one source for all your financial information. You will want to bring this organizer with you to each meeting. It not only organizes all the complex information regarding your plan, but it serves as a resource for you and your family.

For example, one of my long-term clients was a former Baptist minister who lived in the Midwest. When he reached age seventy-five, his health deteriorated. He grew concerned about his family's lack of knowledge regarding his financial plan. During our annual review of his financial plan, he asked, "What do I do about their lack of information?"

I said, "Just give them our phone number. We have copies of everything." When he died, his children called our office, and we brought them up to date on his financial plan. As the financial planning firm for the deceased, we had a complete record of his information. That saved the grieving family countless hours of frustration and anxiety, as well as the trouble and expense of hiring a lawyer to track down all of the details of the pastor's financial life.

During this third session, you also review your overall financial plan. This session will address such issues as whether the existing plan still makes sense. Are other adjustments needed? Are there lingering questions or concerns? This interview usually lasts about an hour. After this third interview, the rest is simply a matter of monitoring the financial plan.

WHAT'S IMPORTANT ABOUT AN ANNUAL REVIEW?

It's unfortunate, but life is much too fluid to create a financial plan that lasts "once and for all." There are no rigid thirty-year decisions, and you will be fortunate if you are able to stay most of the course for five years. On the other hand, if you have created a good, well-thought-out plan with competent professional help, then your goals will be sufficiently elastic to accommodate the ups and downs of real life easily.

Life is dynamic—always changing, always moving, always evolving. Dynamic is an excellent concept to apply to your financial plan. That is why your financial goals will also evolve and change.

A financial plan is alive and active. It grows and matures. It incorporates many different changes along the way. Your goals will change. You might change careers, get married, have children, watch them grow up and leave home, receive an inheritance, take time away from your career, or decide to start your own business. No matter what happens in your life, your financial plan must evolve with you.

Continual changes and innovations in financial products also will require that you have a fresh look at your plan. For example, let's consider a relatively simple instrument like life insurance. Years ago, you could only purchase two types of life insurance—term or whole life. In the late seventies, primarily as a result of the dramatic rise in interest rates, insurance companies unraveled the product. Then they put it back together in very flexible plans. These companies created universal life so the insurance companies could pay a substantially increased rate of interest on the cash value.

By 1985, most insurance companies had converted their whole life contract holders to universal life contracts. Then another evolution occurred. As interest rates began to fall and the stock market began to rise, the product was transformed into variable universal life. Through this new product, investors who purchased life insurance contracts could invest their insurance premiums directly into mutual funds (called separate accounts). This innovative, state-of-the-art life insurance contract provides relatively low-cost insurance for the entirety of a person's life but also allows for substantial investment and tax advantages.

Another reason for an annual review—even if there are no life changes or the financial industry hasn't changed—is that more than likely, the government has introduced new rules regarding financial matters. Congress usually is not stagnant about financial issues, and laws are constantly changing. The tax laws are continually being revised. During the nearly two decades that I have been in the financial planning industry, I can recall about ten significant changes regarding Individual Retirement Accounts alone—and that's not counting all of the other financial instruments.

Change impacts every aspect of your life, including your finances. A financial plan, like your life plan, is a reflection of you. As your life changes, a comprehensive financial plan will help you make the necessary economic adjustments that will accompany those changes.

It is important to remember two key points: First, be responsible and buy the appropriate insurance that will cover your needs. Second, remember that insurance must be purchased before you need it.

CHAPTER 10

Determining How Much
Insurance Is Enough

T he title for this chapter is a perennial question that will be examined in depth through financial planning. In the next few pages, I will examine the various types of insurance. You can use this material to review your personal insurance needs.

Why should so much attention be devoted to the issue of insurance? Because appropriating for the unexpected and making provision for one's family has been a paramount consideration for people throughout the ages. For example, 2000 years ago, the apostle Paul wrote Timothy, "If anyone does not provide for his relatives, and especially for his own family, he has denied the faith and is worse than an unbeliever" (1 Timothy 5:8).

Before you can afford to invest a dollar, first you must protect that dollar. Insurance is the wonderful financial instrument that allows us to exchange a potentially profound and unlimited risk for a reasonable cost (i.e., the premium). Because we can transfer this unlimited liability to an insurance company, we are able to live with the assurance that if something tragic happens, at least we will be financially protected.

Insurance is sometimes maligned as a confusing financial tool. How much do we need? What type should we purchase? How long should we hold a particular type of insurance? What benefits are included in the insurance?

WHY SHOULD YOU HAVE INSURANCE?

Before I cover the specifics of insurance, let me issue a warning: One of the main reasons why our country has so many cultural, political, and economic problems today is precisely because the government is doing something that the founding fathers never intended. As individual citizens, we have failed to take responsibility for accumulating sufficient assets to cover our retirement, and we have failed to protect ourselves from the high cost of healthcare with adequate, self-paid insurance protection.

Many people believe they are entitled to healthcare and retirement benefits through government-created programs. Not only is there a cultural cost to shifting responsibility for our financial welfare to the government, but there is also a huge monetary drain. If these entitlement programs were eliminated from the budget of the United States, our country would not only be able to significantly reduce taxes, but it also could run a continual surplus. For over a decade, almost half of the fiscal budget was earmarked for social welfare programs, and that percentage shows no sign of abating.

In a free society, each person has an individual responsibility to appropriately manage his own insurance and financial plans. That is not the responsibility of the government. If we fail to uphold our individual responsibility, then to the extent of that failure, we contribute to the fiscal (and social) decay of our nation. This warning is little discussed in the media, but each of us bears the responsibility to consider it.

Regarding insurance, it is important to remember two key points. First, be responsible and buy the appropriate insurance that will cover your needs. Second, remember that insurance must be purchased before you need it. Insurance must be secured before the risk it is designed to cover actually occurs. You can't wait until you have an auto accident to buy insurance to cover the accident. Nor can you wait until your physical condition deteriorates before you purchase health insurance. If you are ill, no insurance company can reasonably accept you. The lesson is clear: Apply for insurance before you need it and while you are eligible.

For the sake of simplicity, I will treat each insurance component separately: (1) liability insurance, (2) homeowner and renter insurance, (3) automobile insurance, (4) disability insurance, (5) long-term care insurance, (6)

Medicare supplement insurance, (7) health insurance, and (8) life insurance.

1. Liability Insurance

Lawsuits with heavy financial consequences and personal liability are rampant in the United States. Whether someone trips and falls in your yard, accuses you of slander, gets bitten by your dog, or gets hit by your child, you'd better be prepared to suffer through a lawsuit. All too quickly, a simple mishap can turn into a nightmare. Television commercials that feature various attorneys who advertise their legal prowess remind us that each of us is vulnerable to such litigation. At present, our best option is to protect ourselves with a personal liability policy.

As *The ABC's of Managing Your Money* points out, a "Personal liability umbrella policy will protect you and your family from claims arising out of nonprofessional activities." Author Jonathan Pond, CPA, continues his assertion, "A good umbrella policy will protect you, your family members living in your home, children attending school away from home, and even pets. In addition, the policy should cover legal defense costs, critically important since even the successful defense of a lawsuit can be very costly. The best protection against the threat of a lawsuit is to purchase a personal liability umbrella insurance policy."

This liability insurance policy can be purchased at a reasonable cost, depending on the amount of exposure and coverage. This type of policy should give you peace of mind when you watch those video blooper shows that replay a neighbor's car rolling down the sidewalk without a driver—headed toward the swimming pool across the street.

2. Homeowner and Renter Insurance

Your property insurance should cover unexpected loss to your property. Most policyholders tend to be under-insured. Here are some suggested coverage guidelines:

- Homeowner or renter insurance should cover at least 80 percent of the replacement value of your home, allowing for annual inflation. This coverage will add additional cost to the policy, but it represents a necessary value.

- Your policy also should include replacement-cost coverage for your household contents so that you avoid having to haggle with the insurer over the actual cash value of any losses.

- If you have a special collection, such as jewelry, guns, or paintings, you'll want to add a floater policy to your basic contract. This floater policy will cover the value of the collection that exceeds the minimum allowed through the basic plan.

- Be aware that computer equipment and other material used to operate any business inside the home will necessitate additional coverage.

3. Automobile Insurance

Most automobile insurance policies cover a standard, which meets the minimum needs of most motorists. The following list includes five types of coverage that you will want to make sure are included in your policy.

Bodily Injury Property Liability

This insurance covers injury to pedestrians and occupants of other vehicles and damage that you have done to the property of others. Discuss the proper amount of coverage with your insurance agent, being aware that as you accumulate more assets, you should increase the amount of your insurance.

Medical Payments Insurance

This insurance will cover medical payments on behalf of the policyholder and family members, as well as other passengers in the vehicle. Ask your agent to compare the need for this insurance with what your health insurance policy will cover.

Uninsured Motorist Coverage

Although many states require a minimum amount of liability coverage for any vehicle, some motorists violate this law. Additionally, the minimum required insurance may be less than what is needed to compensate for actual loss. By purchasing this insurance, the policyholder will be covered for both uninsured and underinsured risks from other drivers.

Collision Insurance

This insurance usually is required on any vehicle with a mortgage or lease. It covers damage to the vehicle regardless of who actually caused the loss. If your vehicle is not financed, you may find it more economical to reduce or eliminate this coverage—particularly if your vehicle has little monetary value.

Comprehensive Insurance

This insurance covers your vehicle from virtually all risks including theft, vandalism, collision with animals, and so forth.

4. Disability Insurance

For most working people, the greatest risk probably comes from the loss of income due to a disability. Yet unless the employer provides a good policy, most people do not have nearly sufficient amounts of disability insurance to protect against such a loss.

Disability insurance is designed to replace your lost future wages in the event of an illness or injury. For example, if you are currently earning $40,000 a year and expect to work for another twenty years, adjusting for inflation at 4%, even without any real increase in your salary, you will earn $1,191,123 during this time period.

You and your family will expect at least $1.1 million from your wages over the next twenty years to accomplish your dreams. So if you suddenly became disabled and could not work any longer, your dreams would evaporate. Because an increase in expenses typically accompany a disability, your dreams can be transformed into nightmares for the entire family.

Having some amount of disability insurance, but not the right kind, also can be devastating. I had this fact forever ingrained in my mind with a story I heard shortly after I moved to Nashville. Gary, a thirty-five-year-old husband and father of two, was involved in an accident that paralyzed him from the waist down. Instead of working as a construction foreman, Gary was sitting in a wheelchair. Even though he had suffered this misfortune, Gary was lucky to have survived the accident. And because he had earlier purchased enough disability insurance, his economic lifestyle did not have to change. On the other hand, Gary wasn't so lucky. His benefit period capped out at five years. Gary was already wrestling with a loss of self-worth.

As he faced the termination of his benefits, he grew increasingly distraught. Finally, in the last year of his benefit period, unable to cope with the loss of both his physical abilities and his income, Gary resorted to suicide. He left a note telling his family that he could not bear to watch them suffer the effects of both his physical inability to be a father and husband, and his economic inability to provide for his family.

Disability insurance protects wage earners from adding financial tragedy on top of personal tragedy. Here are some guidelines when shopping for this type of insurance:

- Cover at least 65% of your earnings. If you purchase the policy, any of your benefits from the policy will be tax-free.

- Extend the period of time between when the disability begins and when you can start receiving benefits for as long as your assets will provide for your needs. This coverage will result in reduced premium rates.

- Be sure to add some kind of inflation protection, and update your coverage annually.

- If you are in a specialized field, you may want to add your "own occupation" to the definition of disability. This type of policy will increase your disability insurance expenses, but it will allow you to collect benefits if you cannot perform the primary duties of the job you are working.

5. Long-Term Care Insurance

Like disability insurance, long-term care insurance is designed to protect assets. As the United States population grows increasingly senior, the need will increase for long-term care (LTC) insurance. You cannot depend on

Medicare to cover these expenses. Medicare will not cover the costs associated with long-term convalescent care. Unless you intend to pay upward of $40,000 a year for that care from your own assets, you'll need a well-thought-through LTC insurance policy.

Until the late 1980s, insurance companies had scant actuarial information to establish the baselines for benefits and premiums. This situation has changed drastically today. A number of excellent plans are available from reputable, established insurance companies. In fact, today a long-term insurance plan should be purchased through a "building process." There are numerous benefits that can be built into a plan in order to develop just the right package for any insured. For example, some individuals are quite firm that they never want to enter or be treated in a convalescent home. For these individuals, an LTC plan with the primary benefits weighted toward home healthcare not only will allow them to remain in their home while receiving care, but it also will give them increased peace of mind as they enter their twilight years.

An LTC insurance plan can be customized with many benefits. Because they are too numerous to address here, I'll instead suggest that you use the following guidelines when considering LTC insurance:

- Be sure that you have a sufficient home healthcare provision.

- Extend the coverage for life, not for a period of years.

- Include as few ADL triggers (activities of daily living) benefits as possible.

- Buy LTC insurance early (when you are in your early sixties).

Here is a primary profile of someone who needs this type of insurance. He or she would be approaching retirement with a net worth between $200,000 and $1,000,000. If your net worth is below $200,000, the premiums may be prohibitively expensive when compared to your income. If your net worth is above $1,000,000, it may make more sense to pocket the premium and self-insure. Your individual situation may be different. Seek professional counsel, and involve your children in the decision-making process.

Always remember that you are in the driver's seat. There are almost limitless ways you can arrange benefits to fit your needs. When a salesperson suggests a particular type of LTC policy, don't buy it immediately without some additional research. Contact your state insurance commissioner's office and ask for information about LTC insurance. They will provide you with a pamphlet that details the various features of an LTC policy.

Finally, don't be penny-wise and pound-foolish. What do you need in LTC? Determine this first, and then add benefits that meet your particular goals. For example, let's say you want your insurance to cover your costs for any extended convalescent care. If the average cost for that care in your area is running about $90 per day, don't buy a policy that covers only $65 per day. Additionally, make sure you add an inflation adjustment feature to the policy. Ultimately, you should shop for what you need, not for what you want to pay in premium.

6. Medicare Supplement Insurance

Medicare supplement insurance is designed to cover the gap between what Medicare will pay in medical-care expenses versus what you'll actually be charged. Because this type of insurance varies from state to state and because it is politically sensitive, it changes frequently. I suggest you contact the state insurance commissioner's office and ask for the information pamphlet on Medicare supplement insurance. It will explain why this coverage is necessary for anyone who is a participant in the Medicare insurance program. Also, the pamphlet covers what types of standard policies can be obtained, and how to compare when shopping for this type of insurance.

You also should be aware of the six-month open-enrollment period surrounding your sixty-fifth birthday. During open enrollment, you will be able to apply for this insurance without having to be approved medically. In other words, you cannot be denied this insurance if you apply during this period. If you delay past this six-month window of opportunity, you will have to go through an underwriting process, and it is quite possible that your application will be turned down due to your medical history.

7. Health Insurance

Most Americans have health insurance through their employer. Self-employed workers and those workers who are not covered by a group plan will need to buy an individual policy. There are three types of plans on today's market: HMOs (health maintenance organizations), PPOs (preferred provider organizations), and traditional health plans. HMOs and PPOs will be less expensive than a traditional plan, but the policy usually will not be as flexible or as portable as a traditional plan.

The following are some features that you should make sure are part of your health insurance plan:

- Comprehensive coverage that will cover you wherever you need treatment and for whatever ails you. Stay away from the cheaper policies, which cover only certain types of illnesses or injuries.

- Acceptable and definite maximum out-of-pocket cost. Know the amount of your maximum portion for any catastrophic claim.

- Guaranteed renewable. Reputable insurers have a long history in the industry and sell comprehensive policies. Almost always these comprehensive policies include the provision to be guaranteed renewable.

Never buy solely according to the premium! Health insurance is like everything else in a free market—you get what you pay for. Don't shop for the lowest premium until you: (a) have the policy provisions that you want;

(b) know that you are dealing with a financially secure insurer that has been in the healthcare business for many years; and (c) know that you can be approved medically for the policy.

Here's one final thought about health insurance: If you are self-employed, I strongly encourage you to look into a medical savings account (MSA). The government authorized 750,000 of these accounts as an experiment. An MSA has a high deductible ($2,500 to $15,000), which initially sounds like a disadvantage. However, that high deductible is complemented by a tax-deductible contribution to your medical savings account, so that you have the money to make up for the deductible if you need it.

And here's the great part. If in any year you don't need to use the money you put into the MSA, you get to keep it! And keep in mind that it was already a tax-deductible contribution. The bottom line is that you could end up saving thousands of dollars (toward your retirement or other financial goal) that would have otherwise gone to an insurance company to pay the higher premium associated with low-deductible plans. Now that is more typical of the American way to address high healthcare costs!

8. Life Insurance

I've left life insurance until last for a reason. It's the one type of insurance where people have the greatest emotional ties. They say things like, "I don't believe in whole life insurance" or "You should always buy term insurance and invest the difference" (referring to the lesser cost of term insurance versus the higher cost of whole life).

Understand that the type of life insurance you buy should have no direct connection to your belief system. I believe in God, but I don't ascribe that same level of value to a simple financial instrument. Life insurance is an exceedingly important instrument in most people's financial plan—that's it and nothing more. Let's examine life insurance on an intellectual level rather than on an emotional level. Unfortunately, if you discuss life insurance with an insurance salesperson, then you probably will find yourself pulled into an emotional discussion. Have the courage and insight to recognize this pitfall, then direct the discussion to an intellectual level.

Most people are substantially underinsured. They are underinsured for two basic reasons: (1) They don't know how to calculate their true insurance need; and (2) they think that even if they did know their true need, they couldn't afford that amount of insurance. You can solve these two problems easily, but only after getting rid of your biases. Simply determine your need and then shop for the least expensive way to fulfill the need.

Here's a good rule of thumb: Your life insurance coverage should be between five and ten times your annual earnings. To meet this need, begin to consider annual renewable term insurance. You will be amazed how inexpensively you can provide the amount of financial security that your family deserves.

LOVE AND TAXES

There are two additional considerations before you actually purchase the insurance. The first consideration relates to love and the second relates to taxes.

Life insurance may be considered the greatest love letter you could ever write to your family. If the most traumatic event did occur, if a wage-earning spouse or parent died, the emotional toll on the family would be incalculable. There is no earthly way to mitigate this loss; however, we can substantially eliminate the accompanying financial loss. In fact, I will say that a bread-winner has a responsibility to make adequate provision for the care of his family, even in the event of his or her death.

Many times while discussing the responsibility of life insurance with a couple I will hear, "Oh, she'd get remarried." Or, "He could get a better job." These kinds of responses project unrealistic optimism in the face of a most tragic event. Instead, I've developed a rule about the decision-making process: Before you decide on how much insurance to purchase, assume that you are already dead, sitting with a checkbook in hand, and looking down at your family left on earth. If you could simply, magically write a check and deposit it into your family's account to make sure that the emotional loss was not compounded by economic deprivation, what would be the amount of that check? Whatever your answer, that is the amount of insurance you should own.

Life insurance enjoys very special tax treatment. To the extent that your life insurance has a cash value (savings) portion to it such as whole life or universal life, that savings element of the contract will grow tax-deferred. In other words, you will not have to pay income tax on the gain while it accumulates in the policy. In fact, depending on the type of policy and the method used for accessing the cash value, it is possible to never pay any tax on the earnings. There are some unique tax advantages associated with cash value life insurance. With flexible-premium options and the opportunity to access the cash value virtually on demand, a state-of-the-art cash value insurance policy such as variable universal life can be an excellent cornerstone to a developing financial plan.

Let's illustrate the power of the tax-deferral benefit of a variable universal life policy. You determine to save $300 each month for the next twenty years. Investment A currently is taxable, but investment B is tax-deferred. In this hypothetical example, we'll assume that both investments receive the same rate of return—say 12% annually. If you are in a 28% tax bracket, at the end of twenty years, investment A would be worth $191,443—but investment B would be worth $296,777. The difference amounts to $105,334.

Of course, in the case of life insurance, we also would have to take the cost of the insurance into consideration. In most cases, however, particularly where the intent is to invest the maximum into the policy that tax law allows, even after considering the yearly cost of the policy, the difference in savings associated with tax deferral makes the variable universal life insurance contract an attractive investment option. If you defer the income tax on your investment gain, it can make a tremendous difference in the ending net value.

Whether to use cash value insurance instead of term, which type of cash value insurance to use, and how much to invest are issues well beyond the scope of this chapter. I strongly suggest that you and your financial planner consider this special tax treatment for your life insurance before you determine how to solve your insurance needs. Tax-deferred insurance will also be a factor in addressing your long-term savings program.

Here are some general principles that I have used in the area of life insurance planning with my clients. I see whole life insurance as an expensive, inflexible, and obsolete type of insurance. I recommend some form of straight term insurance or universal life insurance, especially if you are considering an investment plan or if you are in a higher tax bracket.

To really give you some insight into what you can do with life insurance as a financial planning tool, I'll give you a peek at what I personally own. I have a variable universal life policy that offers multiple mutual fund investment choices (referred to as separate accounts). These funds represent multiple asset classes, which I have managed by a portfolio management process based on Modern Portfolio Theory. The policy allows me to access the profit from my investment without ever paying any income tax. This is accomplished through a loan provision.

I can access my invested dollars in the policy on a tax-favored basis through borrowing. And because the policy guarantees that I will never be charged more for the loan than I earn in interest on the borrowed funds, I may be able to keep the money and never make any payments—principal or interest—on the loan. Now that's a life insurance policy! You should know that certain situations could occur to cause the loss of these tax benefits—again underscoring the importance of relying on professional financial planning assistance.

Several years ago I was involved in one of the most interesting applications of this concept. One day a young, single doctor in his mid-thirties came to my office for some financial planning assistance. By most people's standards, this doctor was well-to-do. His investment portfolio approached $1 million, but his income taxes were so high that he felt as if he was spinning his wheels. By the time his loss of personal exemptions and deductions were accounted for, and then both the highest state and federal income tax rate were applied, he was only able to keep about 55 cents of every dollar he made (whether from his investments or wages). I proposed that this doctor fund a variable universal life policy. The tax laws calculate the maximum contribution allowable to a VUL in any year without reducing or eliminating the income tax advantages. In his case, we set up the VUL so that he contributed $90,000 a year. With that amount going in, the death benefit of the policy turned out to be $2,791,574.

Obviously this young, single professional with a million-dollar investment portfolio didn't need that much life insurance. In fact, you could argue that he didn't need any life insurance at all. But he did need income tax help, and the VUL policy gave him such assistance. He did well on the earnings over the next five years, averaging about 12%—and he didn't have to pay a dime of it in taxes!

At the end of the fifth year, he had accumulated over $472,000 in his cash value. Subtracting the $364,000 in premiums he paid during this period, he still gained about $108,000. Now if the same dollars that were invested in the variable universal life policy had been invested instead in, say, a taxable investment averaging the same 12%, the gain would have been only $55,119. And keep in mind that, not only did the young doctor gain an extra $52,000 over the taxable equivalent, but also he had a $2.7 million insurance benefit!

This example is for illustration purposes only. To determine whether a variable universal life policy is in your best interest, you and your financial advisor should carefully review the pros and cons of such a policy.

Here's the bottom line regarding insurance: Commit to purchasing enough life insurance so that if you die prematurely your family will be financially secure. Don't be afraid of the premiums. If you buy the policy when you are healthy, term insurance is very inexpensive. If you choose the more expensive method of providing life insurance benefits through a cash value product such as variable universal life, recognize that there are many creative ways of paying for it that can have a very positive impact on your overall financial plan.

Before I leave the section on life insurance, I want to address one more issue—the question of whether children should have life insurance. I'll give my answer with an incident that happened a few years ago. Early in my career, my employer developed a program that allowed its insureds to convert their whole life policy to the more state-of-the-art universal life policy. In most cases, this was definitely in their best interest. I was contacting all the insureds in my territory about the program.

One of these families had two parents and three little girls. They lived on a farm in rural eastern Colorado, and were, by community standards, of moderate income. I also knew them as members of our church. They considered the program and decided it was something they wanted to do. In the process, I provided each of them with increases in coverage, including the girls. In fact, the small $5,000 policies for the children were converted to $25,000. I remember thinking that amount would be something they could take with them into their new families in the years to come.

About four months later, during Sunday worship service, the pastor began praying for one of the little girls. She had just been diagnosed with leukemia. Startled, I made a mental note to check on the policy to make sure it was issued and in order. Thankfully, everything was in order.

The little girl's condition deteriorated, and the prognosis was not good. Her parents made continuous visits to Denver for the little girl's chemotherapy. Each trip took all day, since drive time alone was five hours, plus the hours at the hospital for treatment and recovery. Eventually, two days turned into four days. The situation got so bad that people in the community and church began helping do the farm chores, including the arduous hand irrigation that had to be done in that dry climate.

One day I stopped by their house to check on them. When I knocked on the white-frame farmhouse door, the mother greeted me and asked me to come inside. As the three little girls played outside on the trampoline, her eyes filled with tears as she began to give me an update. Suddenly, we heard a scream and ran to the door, only to see the sick five-year-old girl jumping on the trampoline, crying at the top of her lungs, "I'm going to die! I'm going to die! I'm going to die!"

The two sisters just watched, and their mother bolted out the door to wrap the poor girl in her comforting arms.

As I silently walked to my car, I saw all four of them in one big family hug, crying and holding each other.

About six months later, the little girl died. Again, I made my way out to that white farmhouse and knocked on the door. The mother and father both came to greet me, but no words were spoken. They knew why I was there. I handed them the check for $25,000 and whispered, "I'm so, so sorry."

The mother, with tears streaming down her face, hugged me and I departed. Later I found out that because the cancer treatment was considered experimental, their health insurance did not cover over $100,000 of their bills. And with the enormous costs of running a farm as an absentee owner, the family was in debt well beyond anything that $25,000 could begin to cover.

So, do I believe children should have insurance? You bet! How much insurance? Enough coverage to cover the funeral and any expenses associated with the parents focusing away from their occupation and on the physical health of their sick child. The insurance should also cover the emotional health of the family—for a long time to come.

Don't skimp on this important area of life insurance. The potential cost of bypassing this coverage is simply much higher than you can imagine.

*Whether a particular investment
should be included in your financial
plan should be dictated more by the
objectives of your individual
situation than by the characteristics
of a particular investment.*

CHAPTER 11

Choosing the Right
Investment Strategy

S everal years ago, a highly successful NCAA coach was referred to me. Jack, along with his wife, Anne, had made a fairly good income over the years and was approaching retirement. Anne was an accountant, and considerably younger than he. His investment program consisted of an employer-provided retirement benefit, an employer-provided defined-contribution plan similar to a 401(k), mutual funds, and individual stocks. He asked me to review his program and make recommendations.

After meeting with him and his wife, I made the following suggestions:

- Purchase a variable universal life insurance policy. This would allow Jack to take the maximum income from his defined-benefit plan at retirement without having to reduce it in order to provide income for Anne in the event he predeceased her (which would be likely). Instead, and if he did predecease her, the life insurance benefit would pick up where the defined benefit left off. In the event that she predeceased him, he would have the option of canceling the insurance and getting the cash value returned to him, or changing the beneficiary to someone else, such as children.

- Reduce the amount currently in their money market mutual fund from $40,000 to $10,000, and move the $30,000 to a managed mutual fund portfolio.

- Move a considerable amount to a combination of investments that are not subject to market risk, such as triple-net-lease real estate programs, tax credit programs, and an oil and gas program. These would not only further diversify his portfolio, but also give him cash flow, and substantial income tax relief—both now and in the future.

- Convert much of the remaining mutual funds and stock portfolio to variable annuities coupled with professional asset allocation. This would reduce his income tax liability on a current basis and for all future years, since he then would be taxed only on what he actually spent, not on what he earned.

With an eye toward retirement, we developed an investment program that reduced his overall risk through diversification, increased his pension income through providing survivor benefits from insurance, substantially reduced his income tax liability for many years to come, and increased his opportunity to achieve a higher return on his portfolio. Jack and Ann were pleased and felt more confident about the future.

The topic of investments is filled with endless categories of opportunities such as stocks, bonds, mutual funds, Individual Retirement Accounts (IRAs), 401(k)s, tax-sheltered annuities, limited partnerships, oil and gas programs, tax credits, gold and precious metals. Add to all the investment options their various income tax consequences, and on top of that all the different types of risk, it is easy to see why people quickly become frustrated. It's difficult to know where to begin, how to tell if you're making the right decisions, and whether you're taking too much risk.

Each of the investments listed in the previous paragraph is neither right nor wrong. Rather, each investment is only appropriate or inappropriate. For example, an investment in a natural gas program, which is considered speculative, would be inappropriate for someone who has no liquidity and little net worth. However, that same natural gas program might be quite an appropriate investment when used as part of a strategy to reduce taxable income for an investor with ample liquidity and a strong net worth, who is suffering from the effects of a sale of taxable, appreciated stock.

Each investment has its own unique characteristics, advantages, and disadvantages. Whether a particular investment should be included in your financial plan should be dictated more by the objectives of your individual situation than by the characteristics of a particular investment. Developing an appropriate investment plan requires a systematic and logical process. Christians, who too often tend to invest emotionally rather than logically, need to remember this principle of appropriateness.

An investor should not purchase a certificate of deposit (CD) simply because it is FDIC (Federal Deposit Insurance Corporation) insured. Similarly, an investor should not refrain from investing in mutual funds simply because their value fluctuates. Rather, the question of whether to invest in either a CD or mutual funds, as well as the questions of when, in what amounts and for what duration, should be approached solely on the basis of your plan objectives. How much money do you need? When do you need it? Will you need it in a lump sum or over a period of time? Should the needs of anyone else be considered? How will this investment be funded—as a single deposit or in monthly installments? What are the income tax considerations?

Consider the process of how you decide to dress yourself each day. Do you say to yourself, "I like flannel shirts, so I'm going to wear a flannel shirt today?" Or do you consider first the weather, and then look at the various options you have for that particular climactic condition? Obviously, if you live in Dallas and it's August, if you decide to wear that flannel shirt, you're going to roast! And so it is with the process of determining how to structure your investment program. Before you say "I like CDs," you should look at the financial climate in which you'll be wearing that CD before you commit to it. What if CDs are only paying 4 percent and you are in a high tax bracket, but you are investing long term? That scenario is just as ridiculous from an investment perspective as wearing a heavy, long-sleeved flannel shirt outdoors on a Dallas summer day!

Do Your Have a Financial Junk Drawer?

The investment portfolio of many people looks like a junk drawer. At home, your junk drawer probably includes various unorganized items like a ruler, a flashlight, a tape measure, a rubber band, and a pencil. You never know what you will find when you open the drawer, because there is little sense of commonality among the items.

Similarly, your investment portfolio might include a savings account, an IRA, a mutual fund, some stock, and an annuity. Let's assume that you purchased each item somewhere along your journey of life for reasons that seemed perfectly logical at the point of purchase. Maybe a friend went into the insurance business, or your father recommended a mutual fund, or your boss suggested a certain stock. Now as you consider your overall investment strategy, you begin to wonder if your program makes sense. You are asking a good question.

INVESTING ON PURPOSE

It has been noted that "The best way to predict the future is to create it." There is only one reason to invest, and that is to provide financial resources to fund your life goals. Although this may sound self-evident, most people fail to check their investment decisions against this touchstone. Instead, they fall into the trap of looking for the "best" investments—without regard to whether they are appropriate to their individual plan.

Let's consider an example of how life goals appropriately dictate investment decisions. For our example, consider the ubiquitous retirement-planning scenario with which most Americans wrestle. Please keep in mind that the actual numbers presented are hypothetical. Each investor needs to consider various risk factors before deciding to invest in any program. There is no assurance that you actually would achieve similar results. Additionally, in the interest of simplifying the examples, income taxes have not been factored into the formulas.

Let's say that your retirement objective is $4,000 a month beginning in twenty years, and that this amount will need to continue for the balance of your life—say thirty years after that. Your first task will be to consider inflation. The $4,000 a month in 2000 is something quite different from an equal amount of purchasing power in twenty years. In fact, after adjusting for an inflation rate of 4%, you will need $8,765 the first month of your retirement if you want the same purchasing power as

$4,000 today! And, because of inflation, that $8,765 minimum monthly income will escalate continuously.

When I present this scenario before a live audience, I usually encounter some degree of disbelief regarding the numbers. Don't take my word for it, just take a look back in time to 1954. In that year, a U.S. first-class postage stamp cost three cents, the average family car could be purchased for just over $2,700, and a loaf of bread cost seventeen cents. The difference between the prices in 1954 and the cost of these same items today is the effect of inflation.

The second task involves adding up all the potential income sources that will be available to help make up your retirement income. These sources may include a company-sponsored retirement plan such as a 401(k), or an individual program such as an IRA. There also may be a pension or annuity benefit. You may or may not want to include Social Security benefits. I am of the opinion that the Social Security system as it exists in 2000 will be dramatically altered within a few years.

Based on current funding and benefit projections, it literally will be impossible for Social Security to pay benefits to me that have been promised (I was born in 1955). Therefore, if you were born in 1950 or later, you may want to eliminate consideration of Social Security benefits from your available retirement income sources. After you have all these projected values, you can subtract this amount from your desired retirement-income of $8,765 per month.

Your third and final task involves accounting for the difference between your desired retirement income and your available retirement income. For example, let's assume your available retirement income will be $5,700 a month. Since your desired monthly income is $8,765, you will need to find a solution for the difference, which is $3,190 per month.

Now we have reached the interesting part of this process. How much money must you accumulate in the next twenty years in order to produce $3,190 a month for the rest of your life? (To simplify this example, we are not adjusting for inflation.) We'll assume a thirty-year post-retirement life. (In other words, the moment you use all your money will be the moment you leave this earth.) The answer to this question will be contingent entirely on the rate of return your retirement savings will be earning. If you are able to achieve a 6% rate of return, you will need to have $534,726 on deposit the day you retire. However, if you are able to achieve an 8% return, you would only need $437,643. A 12% rate of return of would require that you have $313,228 on deposit on the day you retire.

You readily can see what a tremendous difference the rate of return makes on your overall financial position. That impact is even more noticeable if we carry this scenario to the present and consider how much you will need to invest each month between now and your retirement in order to reach your goal.

The means to answering this question relates to the rate of return on your investment. A goal of $534,726 in twenty years will require a monthly investment of $1,157 at a 6% rate of return. If you are able to achieve an 8% return on your investment and have a goal of $437,643, your monthly investment will need to be $743. At 12% with a goal of $313,228, you will need only to invest a manageable $317.

FIGURE 11-1

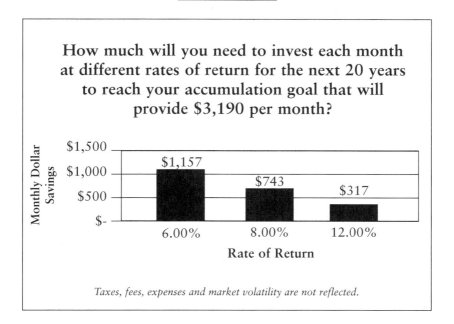

FIGURE 11-2

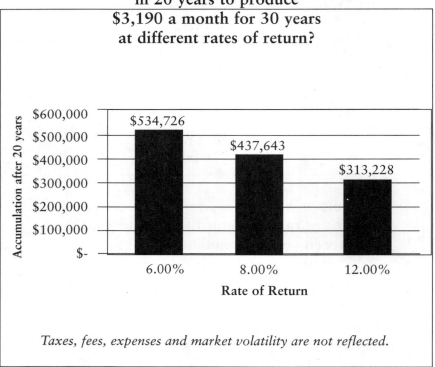

**How much money must you accumulate
in 20 years to produce
$3,190 a month for 30 years
at different rates of return?**

Taxes, fees, expenses and market volatility are not reflected.

Technology now allows investors the opportunity to consider not only what investment return they want to attempt to achieve, but also what values they want to support with their money.

CHAPTER 12

Selecting the
Right Investments

George and Nancy came to my office to talk about their financial plan. They were unsure about the effectiveness of their plan and were looking for a second opinion. One of their investments was in a low-income housing (IRS Code Sec. 42) tax credit program. As a general rule, I like tax credit programs, assuming they meet due diligence requirements and are appropriate for the financial plan of the investor. The problem here was that the couple had invested almost 40 percent of their cash assets in the program, and worse, they had bought the program on an installment plan. This meant that they would pay a high interest rate over ten years on monthly installments just to get some tax credits. To add insult to injury, they were cash strapped, couldn't use all the credits the program was generating, and couldn't liquidate the investment! The only way they ever could make this scenario work was to increase their income—substantially.

In this chapter, I will present a number of popular investment vehicles along with a brief description of each. Consider this information introductory and not comprehensive. My intent is to get you started toward the process of making appropriate investment choices. Before you actually invest, always read the product information carefully and seek professional counsel. I have arbitrarily created five different categories of investment options that exist today: (1) stocks and bonds; (2) mutual funds; (3) variable insurance products; (4) limited partnerships; and (5) bank instruments.

1. Stocks and Bonds

Buying stock is, quite literally, buying a piece (a share) of a corporation. Average Americans began investing frequently in the stock market after World War II. Owning a stock portfolio of blue-chip companies like General Electric® or Ford Motor Company® provided many American households with investment returns to help supplement their retirement income. Today, the percentage of Americans owning stock is greater than at any other time in our history.

If you asked your grandparents how they bought their stocks over the years, they most likely would say, "Through my broker." Although stockbrokers continue to buy-sell-trade in stocks, an increasing number of investors are trading stock on their own, particularly on the Internet. This is not necessarily a good thing. Although investors can save substantially on commissions, they forfeit experience and research in the process.

A form of stock purchase that is becoming more popular, and which probably would not have been included in your grandparents' portfolio, is the initial public offering (IPO). This is one of the riskiest stock purchases you can make, although it could also be the most lucrative. There is so much money in our economy today that a historic opportunity exists for start-up companies to find capital in the market. Technology is creating new methods of developing and meeting consumer demand. Societal and cultural change is dramatic. All of this adds up to new companies producing new goods and services and getting funding by selling part of their company through stock.

I believe that virtually every investment strategy should contain some amount of stock. How much, from what companies, and in what "package" (outright, through a mutual fund, or in a wrap account) is something only you and your advisor will be able to know.

Bonds are the flip side of stock. Buying a bond from a company is the same as lending that company your money. Normally, you'll receive interest (coupon) on the bond, and you may be able to sell it before it matures. If interest rates go down after you purchased the bond, and you decide to sell it, you'll probably make a profit. Conversely, if you decide to sell after interest rates rise, you'll probably not get what you paid for it.

I am not a big fan of buying bonds outright. Corporate bonds can become more or less risky during the time you own them, and you may or may not benefit from that. You may not know about it. Even if the bond's rating doesn't change, the interest-rate environment certainly will, which means that regardless of whether or not you choose to sell during that period, there will be opportunity risk (explained later). Government bonds are safer, but they also pay little interest. That means that if inflation increases, the value of your interest on the bond is reduced. Statistics illustrate that over the course of a decade or more, stocks are a better buy than bonds. Of course, there are always exceptions.

2. Mutual Funds

Mutual funds are by far the most popular investment today for the average American household. From their beginning in 1924, they offered the same advantages as stocks and bonds, without a lot of the risk. The best way to think of mutual funds is as "packaged" stocks and bonds. When you invest in a mutual fund, you hand over your money to the manager of the fund, who looks over the financial landscape and buys, sells, and trades your money in the stock and bond markets for you. You benefit from professional management, diversification, and liquidity, since you can sell (redeem) your shares at will. For all these benefits, you'll have to give back to the mutual fund somewhere between 0.5% to 2.5% of your earnings. Don't let this bother you. A good manager will substantially outperform anything you could do on your own, and will make up some of that difference in lower commissions on trading volume, as well.

Mutual funds are so popular that there are over 10,000 options from which you can select. Each fund will specialize, or focus, on one particular element of economic opportunity. For example, some will invest mostly in companies of a certain size (small capitalization, large capitalization), a certain geography (Far East, Europe, Latin America), specific industry (technology, Internet, health services), and so on. In order to have a proper mutual fund portfolio, I recommend that you invest in several different categories of funds. Optimally, those categories should be determined by the science of Modern Portfolio Theory.

The most important development in mutual fund investing in recent years is the advent of values-based investing. (The particulars of values-based investing have been addressed substantially in Section I.) Technology now allows investors the opportunity to consider not only what investment return they want to attempt, but also what values they want to support with their money. For example, if you suffered through the death of a family member who died of cancer after years of smoking, you may not want your money to be invested in tobacco companies.

Keep in mind that the vast majority of mutual fund managers are not going to consider personal values in their investment process, so you'll need to access technology that will allow you to compare the mutual funds' investments with your values. The Internet site http://www.vfn.net was developed specifically with that capability for comparison in mind.

Mutual funds can be purchased outright or through a number of "wrappers" such as IRAs, 401(k) plans, and insurance products.

3. Variable Insurance Products

The popularity of mutual funds in the 1970s gave birth to a revolution in the insurance industry. Annuities and cash value life insurance, long recognized as poor investment options, gained a new life by using mutual funds (called separate accounts, or subaccounts) to determine investment performance. The consequence of this shift was nothing short of historic. In fewer than fifteen years, variable annuities have grown to over $700 billion in assets. Whereas there were only a handful of insurance companies offering variable products ten years ago, today there are hundreds.

Variable annuities, in their most basic form, are mutual funds wrapped in an annuity. The primary benefit of this marriage is that the investor does not incur income tax on any gain in the mutual funds until that gain is taken out. So the investor benefits from a compounding return on a tax-deferred basis.

This advantage can be substantial. For example, if you were in a 28% tax bracket and you invested $20,000 into an investment that earned 12% over twenty years and were taxed on the earnings each year, your investment would be worth $104,911. By comparison, if you invested the same amount over the same period of time in a variable annuity that had the same return, because you were not taxed along the way your investment would be worth a whopping $192,926. To be fair, there would be mortality expenses on the variable annuity that you might not have on the other investment. So, if we rerun the equation and reduce the 12% return by (the industry average) 1.4% for expenses, you still end up with $150,014.

Variable annuities also have the benefit of insurance in case you die while the stock market is down. Each company's insurance is different, but the idea is that your heirs are protected somewhat in the event the market value of the annuity's mutual funds is below what was originally invested. Some of the disadvantages of variable annuities include surrender charges in the first six to ten years if you decide you want to cash out early, and a 10% tax penalty if you pull money out prior to age fifty-nine and a half.

Variable universal life is similar to variable annuities in that you replace a poorly performing insurance company account with mutual funds to determine investment return. Variable universal life also offers one tax advantage that no other financial instrument offers, and that is the potential to receive all your investment gain entirely tax free. Succinctly put, you can borrow the earnings from the value of your mutual funds in your variable life contract, and since that is technically a loan, it is not considered taxable income by the IRS. This makes it possible to continue to borrow throughout your retirement to supplement your income, and then have the death benefit pay the loan off at your death. Since death proceeds from life insurance policies are generally received free from income tax, you would have paid no tax on the mutual fund earnings during your lifetime, and there would be no tax on the death proceeds either. There are actually some contracts that also offer very low or even no interest on the money you borrow from your contract.

Of course, the above illustration involves a high degree of professional competency. If you are not a financial services professional, you should consult someone with specific competency in this area. There are numerous pitfalls that you would need to avoid when considering such a program.

4. Limited Partnerships

In the early 1980s, limited partnerships were used primarily as tax shelters and only incidentally as economic investments. That all changed with tax reform laws in 1987. In fact, most limited partnerships created prior to the Tax Reform Act of 1986 imploded as a result, causing enormous financial repercussions. Today, limited partnerships primarily offer economic return and only incidental tax advantages.

Because of their volatile past, limited partnerships have taken a beating in the media. In actuality, limited partnerships offer many investment opportunities in real estate, oil and gas exploration, and leasing operations. Whether any limited partnership opportunity is right for you should be determined only after careful examination. These instruments usually have less liquidity than other investment programs, and there is no secondary market such as the New York Stock Exchange to sell it on if you decide you want out.

5. Bank Instruments

The banking industry's share of the investment market has been reduced appropriately in recent years. Banks offer savings accounts, certificates of deposit, and money market funds as typical investment choices. These instruments should not be considered when designing a long-term (five or more years) investment program. Rather, these instruments should be used for short-term needs.

It is unfortunate that so many elderly people still consider the value of FDIC insurance an overriding benefit. It ends up costing them so much that their lifestyle suffers as a result. They forget that the price they pay for that insurance is "opportunity cost;" that is, the amount they could have earned with a different investment. Let's look at this a bit more carefully, because I fear that too many older people are suffering through a less-than-enjoyable retirement for lack of this knowledge.

Jack Grimes wanted guaranteed security. He did not want to be concerned about the market, so at age fifty-five and approaching retirement, Jack moved all his savings ($200,000) into CDs. At age sixty-two, Jack decided to retire and enjoy his remaining years by spending time with his grandchildren. In those seven years prior to retirement, Jack's CDs averaged 5% return and had grown to $281,420. Jack decided he didn't want to touch the principal and would live off of the interest.

Beginning the first month of his retirement, Jack received a monthly check from his bank in the amount of $833.33 ($200,000 x 5% / 12 months = $833.33). Five years into his retirement, Jack began having to cut back on things because inflation was causing prices to go up—but his income remained the same. By age seventy, Jack could barely make ends meet. Ten years after his retirement, Jack could no longer afford to travel by air to see his grandchildren—the price of air travel had become too expensive. All his life Jack had looked forward to enjoying his retirement. Now he knew he could very well reach poverty well before he ran out of time.

If Jack had invested his $200,000 in mutual funds, or variable annuities that returned an average of 12% (admittedly with no guarantees) instead of opting for the low return on an FDIC-guaranteed bank instrument, by the time Jack retired, his account would have been worth

$442,136! The earnings on that account at 12% would have provided Jack a monthly retirement check of $4,421 instead of $833! And because his money was invested in the form of mutual funds, chances are that the underlying value of the funds would have kept pace with inflation.

So next time you hear someone tout the benefit of having money invested in a CD that is backed up by FDIC insurance, remember what that guarantee really costs.

SOME ANSWERS TO YOUR SECRET WISH

Because I've worked in the financial planning industry for almost two decades, I know what you're wanting at this point. Despite all my rhetoric about choosing investments as they apply to your specific life goals and not on their individual characteristics, you likely still have a desire to know what blanket suggestions I may have. You're probably secretly wishing for some kind of benchmark, such as what percent should be invested in what types of investments. Unfortunately, prudent financial planning and investment selection is a highly complex process. Nothing I would suggest should be taken to apply to everyone. I stress that each situation is different. However, here are a few general comments that will help guide you in that process:

- Defer income taxes where possible. Use tax-deferred investments such as variable annuities instead of investments that are currently taxable.

- Be careful not to allocate more than a maximum of 20% of your portfolio to limited partnerships.

- Similarly, use 10% of your portfolio as a benchmark for speculative ventures such as IPOs.

- Consider a variable universal life policy as a fundamental building block in your financial plan. Supplement that with as much term insurance as you need, and put as much cash into the contract's mutual funds as tax law allows.

Use mutual funds as your primary investment strategy. Find a professional who can help you allocate your investment in mutual funds using asset allocation technology.

*With a solid foundation,
you can live each day
on purpose, making a
truly fulfilling life
from all of the resources
that you have.*

EPILOGUE

The sun was not up yet as Libby and I closed the front door and walked toward our car. We buckled our seat belts, and I turned the ignition and backed out of the driveway. We were both very excited, but also equally anxious. We had done this before, almost a year earlier to the day. Libby was almost thirty-seven weeks into her pregnancy, and we had scheduled a C-section for this morning, Friday, August 6, 1999. The actual due date wasn't for another three weeks, but because we never found out why our son, Forrest, died in his last couple of weeks of gestation, the doctors suggested we move the delivery date up.

The drive to Baptist Hospital was uneventful and peaceful. We were both in deep thought and deep prayer. Would something go wrong again? What if it did? Could we handle the devastation of losing another baby right at the end of a normal pregnancy? Almost to the day one year earlier we delivered a stillborn son. It was the most devastating experience our of lives.

We checked into the hospital. Same hallways, same look, a lot of the same faces. I allowed myself a glance at the bed where the last sonogram was done a year earlier, where the doctor pronounced our son dead. Now I watched as nurses came and went from the surgery prep room, sticking, poking, and probing Libby in preparation for the surgery.

Then in came Fred Schwarz, the nurse anesthetist who also happened to be a client of mine. He was there last year, too. Smiling and excited, he moved the IV toward Libby and asked, "Are you hungry? Here comes your breakfast." After skillfully performing his duties, he shut the door and asked if we wanted to join him in a word of prayer. I was so pleased that Fred asked. I had wanted to do the same, but I knew I would choke up as the first words rolled off my lips. We held hands and Fred began. "Lord, we ask you to be with Stephen and Libby at this time of great emotion..."

Things moved rapidly after that, and I put on the surgical coverings and mask. I followed the nurses into the cold surgery room. Fred grabbed a chair and said, "Here, Stephen. Sit right here so you can hold Libby's hand and talk with her." Soon, Dr. Piper and Dr. Schlechter walked in and took control of the room. I looked around and had such a feeling of déjà vu. The exact room, the same anesthesiologist, the same doctors as one year ago. But what about the outcome? Would it be the same?

The doctors and nurses began. It was not long before Dr. Piper joyously announced that we were close, and sure enough, momentarily thereafter, I watched as my daughter was born! The room erupted with cries of excitement and relief, and Ann-Rachel Darling Bolt announced her life with a cry, the most wonderful cry I ever will hear. I was beyond emotion. I was stunned.

The nurses allowed Libby only a few seconds to see her daughter before they raced her out to neonatal care. As Libby was wheeled to her recovery room, I walked out and down the hall, still in my surgical clothes. I looked up and saw Phyllis Keller, Libby's mother, and Ruby. Phyllis excitedly and anxiously asked, "Is everything all right? Is Libby okay? What about the baby?"

I was so caught up with emotion that I had tears in my eyes and couldn't talk. This only made Libby's mother even more anxious. Finally, I was able to whisper, "Yes, Libby is fine."

At this Phyllis said, "What about the baby? Is she all right?" All I could do was nod. At that, all three of us embraced tightly.

Libby and I were able to spend some quality time in her hospital room enjoying each other and the new life with which God had blessed us. One evening, as Libby lay resting and Ann-Rachel was nestled warmly in my arms, I relaxed into the peace and comfort of the moment. I settled back into a soft chair. I looked down at the face of our beautiful child. My mind wandered, and I began thinking about this tiny baby, only two days old, growing into a toddler, a child, a young adult, and then having a family of her own. I thought about what I could do as a trusted parent to help her in that life. What important principles would I teach her?

More than anything else, I will teach her about values. Life is nothing if it is not about values—choices, noise, competing ideas, temptations, frustration, pressure, stress—these are part of life too, unavoidable consequences of living in this world. But as a Christian, I will also teach Ann-Rachel that regardless of the failings of her parents and her friends, and regardless of the troubles, heartache, and sin she will face in her life, God will never, ever leave her. He will always be with her, always perfect, always in love with her.

It is from the vastness of this supernatural love that Ann-Rachel will learn how to live a life of purpose, so that she can reflect the image of this wonderful God in all her life. The power of the Almighty God that created the universe is the same power who nurtures us in life and gives us the power to live life on purpose.

Will Ann-Rachel choose to be a doctor, a teacher, a homemaker? What will her interests and avocations be? How much money will she need, and when will she need it? The answers to these questions are for her to make, and she has the freedom and power to develop her life however she pleases.

These issues will be the foundation from which she will develop her life. And the result of her soul-searching will create the need for her to manage her financial resources in a way that provides sufficient money. I hope to serve Ann-Rachel as her consultant, helping her to weave her own life of purpose and meaning, taking into account first her talents, adding to those her interests, and then finally helping her consider her opportunities. I will counsel her to develop a specific financial plan to support that life, and I'll show her how to manage it in tandem with her changing life goals, so that her life goals and her financial plan are always synchronized.

Finally, I will counsel her to think about how reflecting her values goes well beyond her own life. How her money is invested ultimately will fund somebody's values, so I'll teach her to invest her money to reflect her own values. Money is the economic oxygen of business, and if she is not careful, she will unwittingly provide oxygen to a values and belief system that may be in total contradiction to that of her own.

What would I like for my tiny seven-pound, two-and-one-half-ounce little girl ultimately to do or be in her life? What about her life choices would satisfy me, her caring father? That answer is actually quite simple. My satisfaction will overflow regardless of what she chooses in her life, so long as those choices reflect purpose. Choosing to live a life on purpose begins with a life of faith and conviction and follows with choices based on stewardship, managing resources, opportunities, and time in ways that reflect the character of our awesome God. That life is the ultimate life.

I have similar aspirations for everyone who reads this book. As you have read through the pages of this book, I hope it has triggered you to revisit your own purpose in life, starting with the right foundation. With a solid foundation, you can live each day on purpose, making a truly fulfilling life from all of the resources that you have. If you don't make the conscious decision to be proactive, then in effect you will have made the choice simply to exist. Remember, the right order is *life, purpose, plan, money*. After all, the way you organize *your money* and *your values* ultimately determines the quality of *your life*.

*The dollars you invest will
support businesses in various
industries, many of which may not
be consistent with your personal
values (such as abortion,
pornography, gambling, tobacco).*

Personal Information Form

OBJECTIVES AND RESOURCES

I. RETIREMENT PLANNING
If you retired today, what
  monthly income would you want? $ _____
Age when you desire to retire   _____
Age when your spouse desires to retire   _____

II. COLLEGE FUNDING
Amount you expect to contribute
per child per year for college $ _____

INCOME INFORMATION

Client Earned Income—Self-Employed?
  Yes_____ No____ $ _____

Spouse Earned Income—Self-Employed?
  Yes_____ No____ $ _____

Client Social Security Income $_____
Spouse Social Security Income $_____
Interest/Dividends $_____
Rental Property Gain (Loss) $_____
Other Income $_____
Deductions $_____
Exemptions $_____

Filing Status: ___Single   ___Married-Joint
                        ___Married-Separated
                        ___Head of Household

Current Year Projected Income $ _____
                              Client $ _____
                              Spouse $ _____

LIFE INSURANCE

1. Company   _____
   *Type   _____
   Insured/Owner   _____
   Beneficiary   _____
   Face Amount $ _____
   Annual Premium $ _____
   Loans $ _____
   Current Cash Value $ _____

2. Company _____
   *Type _____
   Insured/Owner   _____
   Beneficiary   _____
   Face Amount $ _____
   Annual Premium $ _____
   Loans $ _____
   Current Cash Value $ _____

3. Company _____
   *Type _____
   Insured/Owner   _____
   Beneficiary   _____

Face Amount $ _____

Annual Premium $ _____

Loans $ _____

Current Cash Value $ _____

4.   Company _____
       *Type _____
     Insured/Owner _____
     Beneficiary _____
     Face Amount $ _____
     Annual Premium $ _____
     Loans $ _____
     Current Cash Value $ _____

DISABILITY INSURANCE

Company   _____
Insured   _____
Annual Premium $ _____
Monthly Benefit $ _____
Waiting Period   _____
Benefit Duration   _____

OTHER INSURANCE

Health

Company   _____
Annual premium   _____
Insured   _____
Coverage Type   _____
Coinsurance %   _____
Max Out-of-Pocket $

*W=Whole Life F=Fixed V=Variable Universal Life T=Term

Lifetime Limit $ _____
Deduct./Person $ _____
Deduct./Family $ _____

Personal Liability

Company   _____
Annual Premium $ _____
Max Coverage $ _____
Deductible $ _____

Medical Supplement

Company   _____
Annual Premium $ _____

Nursing Home/Long-Term Care

Company   _____
Annual Premium $ _____

INVESTMENT ASSETS

Asset Name   _____
     *Type   _____
Owner   _____
Current Value $ _____
Monthly Addition $ _____
Rate of Return   _____
Maturity Date   _____
Current Cash Value $ _____
Notes _____

Asset Name   _____
     *Type   _____
Owner   _____

Current Value $ _____

Monthly Addition $ _____

Rate of Return   _____

Maturity Date   _____

Current Cash Value $ _____

Notes _____

Asset Name   _____

    *Type   _____

Owner   _____

Current Value $ _____

Monthly Addition $ _____

Rate of Return   _____

Maturity Date   _____

Current Cash Value $ _____

Notes _____

Asset Name   _____

    *Type   _____

Owner   _____

Current Value $ _____

Monthly Addition $ _____

Rate of Return   _____

Maturity Date   _____

Current Cash Value $ _____

Notes _____

Asset Name   _____

    *Type   _____

Owner   _____

Current Value $ _____

Monthly Addition $ _____

Rate of Return _____

Maturity Date _____

Current Cash Value $ _____

Notes _____

Asset Name _____

*Type _____

Owner _____

Current Value $ _____

Monthly Addition $ _____

Rate of Return _____

Maturity Date _____

Current Cash Value $ _____

Notes _____

Asset Name _____

*Type _____

Owner _____

Current Value $ _____

Monthly Addition $ _____

Rate of Return _____

Maturity Date _____

Current Cash Value $ _____

Notes _____

* 1=Savings/Checking   2=Certificate of Deposit,
  3=Fixed Annuity   5=Bonds
  6=Notes Receivable   7=Energy (Oil, Gas)
  8=Stocks   9=Mutual Funds
  10=Land   11=Rental Real Estate
  12=Agriculture   13=Gold/Silver/Gems/Coins,
  14=Business,   15=Other

RETIREMENT ASSETS

Asset Name _____
*Type _____
Owner _____
Account Balance $ _____
Ongoing Cont. or % of Pay _____
Rate of Return _____
Notes _____

Asset Name _____
*Type _____
Owner _____
Account Balance $ _____
Ongoing Cont. or % of Pay _____
Rate of Return _____
Notes _____

Asset Name _____
*Type _____
Owner _____
Account Balance $ _____
Ongoing Cont. or % of Pay _____
Rate of Return _____
Notes _____

* I=IRA, E=SEP, K=KEOGH, F=401(K), P=Pension/Profit Sharing, D=Deferred Comp, S=Salary Savings, O=Other, R=Roth, M=Simple

Client: Do you receive company match?
    Yes____ No____

Spouse: Do you receive company match?
    Yes____ No____

MISCELLANEOUS AND PERSONAL ASSETS

Residence _____

Owner _____

Market Value $ _____

Notes _____

Personal Property _____

Owner _____

Market Value $ _____

Notes _____

RVs/Boats _____

Owner _____

Market Value $ _____

Notes _____

Autos _____

Owner _____

Market Value $ _____

Notes _____

Other _____

Owner _____

Market Value $ _____

Notes _____

Other _____

Owner _____

Market Value $ _____

Notes _____

DEBTS

Owner (Home Loan) _____
Current Balance $ _____
Monthly Payment $ _____
Original Amount Financed $ _____
Interest Rate _____
Date Opened _____
Original Term _____

Owner (Home Equity Loan)_____
Current Balance $ _____
Monthly Payment $ _____
Original Amount Financed $ _____
Interest Rate _____
Date Opened _____
Original Term _____

Owner (Investment Loan) _____
Current Balance $ _____
Monthly Payment $ _____
Original Amount Financed $ _____
Interest Rate _____
Date Opened _____
Original Term _____

Owner (Charge Cards) _____
Current Balance $ _____
Monthly Payment $ _____
Original Amount Financed $ _____
Interest Rate _____
Date Opened _____
Original Term _____

Owner (Personal Loan) _____

Current Balance $ _____

Monthly Payment $ _____

Original Amount Financed $ _____

Interest Rate _____

Date Opened _____

Original Term _____

Owner (Auto Loan) _____

Current Balance $ _____

Monthly Payment $ _____

Original Amount Financed $ _____

Interest Rate _____

Date Opened _____

Original Term _____

Owner (Other) _____

Current Balance $ _____

Monthly Payment $ _____

Original Amount Financed $ _____

Interest Rate _____

Date Opened _____

Original Term _____

Does your monthly home loan payment include escrow for taxes
and insurance? Yes_____ No____

Amount of real estate taxes per year

$_____

LIVING EXPENSES WORKSHEET

Auto—Gas	$
Auto—Maintenance	$
Auto—Insurance	$
Homeowners Insurance	$
House—Maintenance	$
Rent	$
Utilities	$
Food	$
Clothing	$
Entertainment	$
Allowances	$
Child Support	$
Childcare	$
Education	$
Fees/Dues/Memberships	$
Gifts	$
Vacations	$
Contribution/Tithe	$
Personal Care	$
Accounting/Legal Fees	$
Out-of-Pocket Medical	$
Pets	$
Other	$
_____	$
_____	$
_____	$
_____	$
Total	$

*With a solid foundation,
you can live each day
on purpose, making a
truly fulfilling life
from all of the resources
that you have.*

APPENDIX B

Risk Profile Questionnaire

Name: _____

Home Address: _____

_____

_____

Home Phone: _____ Home Fax: _____
Date of Birth: _____ S.S./Tax ID: _____
Occupation: _____
Employer: _____
Work Address: _____

_____

_____

Work Phone: _____ Work Fax: _____

Spouse's Name: _____
Date of Birth: _____ S.S./Tax ID: _____
Occupation: _____ Employer: _____

245

Children or Dependents:

Name _____ Birth Date _____

Name _____ Birth Date _____

Name _____ Birth Date _____

Annual Income: $ _____

Estimated Net Worth: $ _____

Estimated Tax Bracket: $ _____

I. CLIENT PROFILE
WHAT TYPE OF INVESTOR ARE YOU?

Determining your personal risk tolerance and expected rates of return are essential in establishing your investment objectives. Therefore, we need your input, which will provide us with the foundation for (a) determining your investment objectives, (b) identifying your risk tolerance, and (c) understanding your performance expectations.

Effective communication is vital in effective investment management. The more we know about you, your current financial situation, and goals, the better strategies we can identify. Your investment portfolio will be customized and tailored to your personal goals and objectives and specifically allocated based on the facts and preferences you provide in the pages that follow.

1. What is the approximate amount of assets to be initially invested? $ _____

2. How are these assets currently being managed?

_____

_____

_____

3. Please indicate the intended use of your investment portfolio.

____Wealth-Building   ____ Future Capital
                                      Expenditures
____Current Income   (Residence, etc.)
____Dependents' Education   ____ Purchasing
                                      Power
____Satisfy Investment Policy   (Maintenance)
____Retirement   ____ Other

_____

_____

4. What percentage of your total investable assets will be represented by this portfolio? (This is vital information in compiling your asset allocation analysis.)

____75% to 100%   ____25% to 50%
____50% to 75%   ____Less than 25%

If known, please indicate the exact percentage: ____

5. Please describe the general composition of your current overall portfolio (including principal residence):

Bank Accounts	$ _____
CDs	$ _____
Money Market Funds	$ _____
Stocks	$ _____
Bonds	$ _____
Mutual Funds	$ _____
Tax-Deferred Annuities	$ _____
Life Insurance (Cash Value)	$ _____
Investment Real Estate	$ _____
Other (Please Specify)	$ _____

6. From your answer on #5, please indicate the split among the following types of accounts:

* Personal Nonretirement Accounts	$ _____
* Retirement Accounts	
IRA/IRA Rollover	$ _____
KEOGH	$ _____
SEP	$ _____
401(k)/403(b)	$ _____
Other	$ _____

7. Are there any constraints on your portfolio with regard to legal or tax consequences?

No_____ Yes_____

If yes, please explain: _____

_____

_____

8. Please estimate the contributions and/or withdrawals, if any, you anticipate making to your portfolio:

Year	Contributions	Withdrawals
1	$ _____	$_____
2	$ _____	$_____
3	$ _____	$_____
4	$ _____	$_____
5	$ _____	$_____

II. INVESTMENT POLICY
NONFINANCIAL CRITERIA

Investments are the economic oxygen of business. The dollars you invest will support businesses in various industries, many of which may not be consistent with your personal values (such as abortion, pornography, gambling, tobacco).

• Would you like your personal values reflected in your investments?

If so, please indicate in general terms if those values are socially conservative or liberal. _____

Below is a list of values issues. Please indicate which issues are important to you in the composition of your investments.

SOCIALLY CONSERVATIVE

Include	Exclude	N/A	
____	____	____	Alcohol/Production and Distribution
____	____	____	Fetal Research/Genetic Engineering
____	____	____	Gambling
____	____	____	Abortion
____	____	____	Pornography
____	____	____	Tobacco
____	____	____	Same-Sex Lifestyle

SOCIALLY LIBERAL

____	____	____	Military Contractors
____	____	____	Environmentally Proactive
____	____	____	Animal Testing/Research
____	____	____	Management: Minority Pro-active
____	____	____	Nuclear Energy
____	____	____	Fossil Fuel Production
____	____	____	Alternative Energy

III. INVESTMENT OBJECTIVE, RISK, TIME, AND RETURN EXPECTATIONS

A. Investment Objective

Your investment objective summarizes the primary purpose of your investment portfolio. It serves to define how your assets should be managed. While asking yourself, "What do I want to accomplish with my investments?" check the on objective which best fits your purpose for investing.

_____ Preserve Asset Value

_____ Generate High Current Income

_____ Achieve Asset Growth with Moderate Current Income

_____ Achieve Strong Asset Growth with Nominal Income

_____ Achieve Maximum Asset Appreciation

B. Risk Tolerance

Investing in different asset classes and asset allocations can result in varying and occasionally wide fluctuations in the value of your portfolio over time. As a general rule, the more risk you are willing to accept, or the more volatility you can withstand, the higher the prospective rate of return you should be compensated with over a sufficiently long time horizon.

Use the following ranges of volatility over a one-year time horizon to help determine a benchmark for the amount of risk you can tolerate, while keeping in mind the investment objective you determined in section A: Investment Objective.

	Upside/ Downside	Potential Variance	Risk Tolerance Potential
_____	5%	0-5%	Very Low
_____	10%	5-10%	Low
_____	15%	10-15%	Moderate
_____	20%	15-20%	Moderate-High
_____	Over 20%	Over 20%	High

C. Time Horizon

Your age and investment time horizon are important variables to consider when constructing your portfolio. Your portfolio should be considered within the context of a longer-term investment horizon. For example, for younger investors, a longer time frame enables them to benefit from strategies that may take many market cycles to be successful while undertaking greater risk. Conversely, investors near on in retirement may want to be more conservative in their investment selections to benefit from low investment risk. A specific time frame is also useful as a benchmark by which investment result can be assessed. With this in mind, place a mark next to the time frame that best corresponds to your profile.

_____   0 - 1 Years __ 1 - 2 Years
_____   2 - 4 Years __ 4 - 6 Years
_____   Over 6 Years

D. RETURN EXPECTATIONS

Construction of a strategic asset allocation is based upon your profile in regard to objective, risk tolerance, and time horizon, but is primarily driven by your expectations of performance. For example, it is not likely to construct an efficient portfolio with an objective of high current income, low risk tolerance and a two-year time horizon, where your return exception is greater than 15 percent.

Likewise, you are shortchanging your portfolio if you have an objective of maximizing asset growth, a high tolerance for risk and a ten-year time horizon, while only expecting an annual rate return of 5%. To set a benchmark, select from the following range of returns the range that best describes your target rate of return on your portfolio, without considering inflation and taxes, in light of your responses to the other profile questions.

____   5% to 7%
____   7% to 9%
____   9% to 11%
____   11% to 13%
____   Other : _____%

Bottom line is that you should always try to earn as high a return as you can with your long-term investing, while at the same time not take any unnecessary risk. Everyone needs a planned strategy for investments. Otherwise, the strategy that you end up with will have only coincidental relevance to your life plan. I am reminded of the political adage, "If you don't stand for something, you'll fall for anything."

Similarly, if you don't hold to an investment plan, you'll end up being courted by every type of investment philosophy that crosses your path. And that can be very dangerous.

*After all, your money
is being used to
support somebody's values
and we think they
should be yours!*

What Is Values-based Investing?

• Does smoking really get on your nerves?

• Are you anti-abortion?

• Does the name Three Mile Island still give you shivers?

So, after you've answered those questions—how about these?

• Is your money invested in the tobacco industry?

• What about companies involved in abortion?

• Nuclear energy?

• Or any number of personal values and issues you care about?

Chances are you probably don't know whether your mutual fund, 401(k) allocation, IRA, variable annuity or variable universal life invests in companies that represent or conflict with your personal values. Don't feel bad. Millions of investors don't and do not have the time to check. That's why we've created moneyand-values.com, the first investor tool that analyzes your current portfolio and finds investments you'll feel good about as a person and investor.

This is values-based investing—matching your personal values and issues with your money and not giving up a thing in performance. After all, your money is being used to support somebody's values and we think they should be yours! And we're not alone.

Research from the Social Investment Forum shows:

- In 1999, over $1 trillion was invested by mutual funds and other investments that utilize some values criteria, by screening for issues such as tobacco, abortion, nuclear power, environment, etc.

- More than 13% of all money that is invested in the U.S. today utilizes some form of values screening.

- Values-based investing has become the most popular form of investing, outpacing traditional investing 2-to-1.

- Studies have proven that values-based investing is just as effective in terms of performance as traditional non-screened investments.

"How Do I Find the Values that Are Reflected in My Investments?"

Moneyandvalues.com's screening instrument allows investors to examine their investments by choosing from

10 different issues that span the political, social and personal values spectrum. The screening tool provides the percentage your mutual fund, 401 (k) allocation, IRA, variable annuity or variable universal life has invested in gambling, pornography or other issues. Whether you consider yourself liberal, conservative or moderate, these primary issues help you to align your money with your values.

Moneyandvalues.com helps you apply values-based investing by choosing from these issues:

Abortion—Takes into consideration companies that manufacture or distribute abortion-causing drugs, hospitals that perform elective abortions, health care plans that cover abortions and corporate contributions to organizations that perform abortions.

Pornography—Takes into consideration companies that manufacture or distribute pornographic material, adult cabaret businesses and advertisers in pornographic magazines.

Gambling—Takes into consideration casinos, lotteries and manufacturers of commercial gaming equipment.

Tobacco—Takes into consideration tobacco growers, processors and manufacturers, as well as tobacco wholesale distributors.

Alcohol—Takes into consideration alcohol producers and wholesale distributors.

Same-Sex Lifestyles—Takes into consideration companies with activities or corporate policies that institutionalize or promote same-sex lifestyles.

Environment—Takes into consideration companies' environmental performances. May also consider superfund sites, toxic emissions, oil and chemical spills and fines.

Nuclear Power—Takes into consideration companies that own or operate nuclear plants. May also consider companies licensed to make nuclear reactors, process nuclear fuel, transport nuclear waste or provide related goods and services to the nuclear power industry.

Defense Contracting—Takes into consideration companies that contract with the federal government to provide lethal weapons for defense purposes.

Affirmative Action—Takes into consideration corporate board and employment diversity policies.

MAKING MONEYANDVALUES.COM
WORK FOR YOU

Moneyandvalues.com is values-based investing in action. Once you have screened your investments, MoneyAndValues.com takes the next step by offering individuals a variety of investments from mutual funds and 401 (k) plans to annuities and IRAs to universal life, that match their values. Through our Values Financial Network, you will be able to discuss your options with a financial advisor who can help find the investments that work for you from a values standpoint and from a real-world financial perspective.

To begin, simply have available the specific names of the mutual funds which you want screened and start the experience by logging onto http://www.moneyandvalues.com and see how simple it is to be assured that your investments really reflect your values.

*Whether mutual funds,
variable annuities or life insurance,
choosing the appropriate
instrument and investing the
right amount of money are
critical success factors.*

APPENDIX D

Integrating Money and Values into Your Financial Plan

There may be two ways that you can reflect your values in your investment decisions depending on the particular investment:

You are able to eliminate from your investments those businesses which represent values that are inconsistent with your own such as companies involved in the production and distribution of pornography, or companies that have a poor environmental record (See the Personal Values Profile).

Some financial services companies offer investors the opportunity to direct a portion of the financial contributions that are made by the company on the investor's behalf. These contributions would go to organizations that fit the values identified in the Personal Values Profiles.

Your financial adviser will assist you in designing a financial plan that reflects your values. He or she likely will use the following process:

**Discuss Financial
Planning Issues**

———————————————————*Review Financial Issues,
Needs, Goals, Taxes, etc.*

**Discuss
Personal Values**

———————————————*Choose values from
Personal Values Profile*

**Develop
Financial Plan**

———————————————*Select Appropriate
Investment Options such
as IRA, Variable Annuity,
Mutual Funds, etc.*

**Apply Money
and Values Program**

———————————————*Apply Screened
Investment Allocation Programs,
Invest in Values-based Mutual Funds,
and/or Complete Affinity Program Forms.*

In order to reach specific investment goals such as retirement, college education funding, or the ability to buy a second home, an investor must be selective in choosing the right financial instruments. Whether mutual funds, variable annuities or life insurance, choosing the appropriate instrument and investing the right amount of money are critical success factors.

Making sure that your investments are appropriate to your financial objectives is only the first of a two step process. The final step involves making sure that your personal values are reflected in the way that your money is invested. For a growing number of people, achieving financial objectives at the expense of their personal values is simply unacceptable. Research from the Social Investment Forum shows:

- In 1999, over $1 trillion was invested in mutual funds and other investments that utilized some values criteria, screening for issues such as tobacco, abortion, nuclear power, environment, etc.

- Over 13% of all money that is invested in the U.S. today utilizes some form of values screening.

- Values-based investing has become the most popular form of investing, outpacing traditional investing by 2-to-1.

The Money and Values Program was developed by Values Financial Network (VFN) to help people maintain the integrity of their personal values while investing their money into mutual funds, privately managed accounts, annuities and other financial instruments.

Your money is akin to being the economic oxygen of business. Where there is money, business can thrive. When you invest, your money helps support some business' values system; the Money and Values Program helps you make sure that values system is your own.

Life is about values. Investing is about reaching financial goals. The two should not be exclusive propositions. Expressing your values in your family, religious institution and politics has always been your unalienable American right. And now you can also express those same values in how you invest.

APPLYING YOUR VALUES

Research on corporate America is provided by research organizations such as Values Investment Forum (http://www.valuesforum.com) and IRRC (http://www. irrc.org).

This information is then provided to investment management companies to be synthesized in a way that can be applied to mutual funds, variable annuities, variable universal life, and privately managed accounts. For more information regarding specific application please refer to the information provided by the particular investment you are considering.

COMMONLY ASKED QUESTIONS

1. How do I tell my advisor what my values are?

Your adviser will present you with a list of ten different issues that you can choose from and these will help build your Personal Values Profile (please refer to the Personal Values Profile form). Although your advisor will attempt to consider all of the values that are important to you, due to constraints beyond the adviser's control, it may not be possible to reflect all of those values in every financial instrument in a way that precisely matches your Personal Values Profile. However, your adviser has received the training necessary to provide you a professional approach in finding the best match available.

2. Can my values be reflected in all of my investments?

That depends on your specific situation. Money and Values can be applied to certain mutual funds, variable annuities, fixed annuities, variable universal life, privately managed accounts, and 401(k) plans. If your situation requires other financial instruments, ask your Money and Values adviser.

3. By aligning my money with my values, should I expect the performance of my investments to suffer?

No. Many studies have been done on this question and the consensus is that there should not be any reduction in the performance of your financial instrument simply on the basis of it being managed to reflect your values. For more complete information on this question you may want to refer to the Social Investment Forum, or Morningstar.

4. Are there additional fees associated with aligning my money with my values?

In most cases the answer is no. With regard to mutual funds, depending on how they are priced, there may be a small charge for the screening service. Always refer to the investment brochure, or prospectus for specific information on any fees, or expenses.

5. If my values change, can I adjust my Personal Values Profile?

Yes. An allocation program used for mutual funds, 401(k) plans and variable products will generally offer more than one Personal Values Profile to choose from. Privately managed accounts are very flexible and can adapt to most changes in screening criteria easily. In the case of specific mutual funds, however, a substantial change in your Personal Values Profile may require that you redeem your shares and purchase different funds.

6. Can I change my mind and discontinue the Money and Values Program?

Yes. You may discontinue the Money and Values Program at any time and without any associated fee. Of course, if you choose to redeem shares, liquidate your investment, or surrender a contract there may be certain expenses incurred as a result. Please refer to the product information for more specific information.

7. Can I wait and apply the Money and Values Program at a later date?

That depends. Each situation is different. The best time to apply your values to your investments is before you invest your money, or reposition your assets.

8. Why would someone want to align their money with their values?

For the same reason that people exercise their right to vote. Voting for the candidate of your choice allows you to apply the political power you have as a United States citizen. Similarly, choosing to invest your money in a way that reflects your values leverages the economic power you have as an investor. Ultimately, your invested money will play a supporting role in some values system; the only question is whether that values system will be yours, or somebody else's.

9. I am only one person, can my money really make a difference?

It is true that few people have enough money to affect a change in corporate values on their own. However, when people who share similar values all decide to exercise their economic muscle, an impact on corporate values can certainly be made. Additionally, many people simply want to maintain the integrity of their own values system by investing their money consistent with their values, regardless of whether it ever affect corporate values.

10. Do all financial advisors offer the Money and Values Program as an integral part of their practice?

No. The only financial advisers certified to offer Money and Values are those who have completed specific training and subsequently passed an examination.

11. Why doesn't everyone align their money with their values?

Although there will always be people who simply don't care where their money is invested so long as they achieve the anticipated return, research indicates that a strong majority of people do prefer to align their money with their values when given the option. For example, according to a study by Yankelovich Partners as reported in a 1999 issue of Pension and Investment News, seven out of ten people would choose to invest in a socially responsible manner in the 401(k) plan if they were given that option.

As technology continues to expand investors' abilities to control where their money goes, values-based investing will become accessible to an increasing number of people. That is why it is the fastest growing part of the investment industry today.

PERSONAL VALUES PROFILE

Please choose from the following issues by placing a check next to each one that you would like considered in your investment program.

1. **Abortion**—Takes into consideration companies that manufacture or distribute abortion causing drugs, hospitals which perform elective abortions, health care plans which cover abortions and corporate contributions to organizations that perform abortions.

2. **Pornography**—Takes into consideration companies that manufacture or distribute pornographic material, adult cabaret businesses and advertisers in pornographic magazines.

3. **Gambling**—Takes into consideration casinos, lotteries, manufacturers of commercial gaming equipment.

4. **Tobacco**—Takes into consideration tobacco growers, processors and manufacturers as well as tobacco wholesale distributors.

5. **Alcohol**—Takes into consideration alcohol producers and wholesale distributors.

6. **Same-Sex Lifestyles**—Takes into consideration companies with activities or corporate policies that institutionalize same-sex lifestyles.

7. **Environment**—Takes into consideration companies' environmental performance. Also may consider superfund sites, toxic emissions, oil and chemical spills and fines.

8. **Nuclear Power**—Takes into consideration companies that own or operate nuclear plants. Also may consider companies licensed to make nuclear reactors, process nuclear fuel, transport nuclear waste or provide related goods and services to the nuclear power industry.

9. **Defense Contracting**—Takes into consideration companies that contract with the federal government to provide lethal weapons for defense purposes.

10. **Affirmative Action**—Takes into consideration corporate board and employment diversity policies.

For more information, contact:
Values Financial Network, Inc.
2505 21st Avenue South, Suite 204
Nashville, Tennessee 37212
888 FIN-VALU (346-8258)
Fax: (615) 383-7804